THE FLOSS ON THE MILL

To Denys and Martha,
for their help and love,
and for giving me the confidence
to go on with the project
through thick and thin,
no matter what.

the *f*loss on the *m*ill

THE RE-AWAKENING OF A WATERMILL

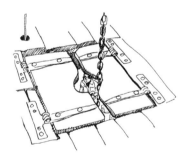

Desna Greenhow

ILLUSTRATED BY JED FALBY

First published in the United Kingdom in 2004 by
The Hobnob Press, PO Box 1838, East Knoyle, Salisbury SP3 6FA

British Library Cataloguing in Publication Data
A catalogue record for this book is available from the British Library.

ISBN 0-946418-20-9

Typeset in 11/15 pt Scala
Typesetting and origination by John Chandler
Printed in Great Britain by Salisbury Printing Company Ltd, Salisbury

Contents

I am very grateful to the following friends, for their encouragement and support:-
Peter & Joan Speke, Christopher Holdsworth, Detta Fane-Trefusis, Glencairn & Jenny
Balfour-Paul, Peter & Susie Barrett, Barbara Farquarson, Peggy Larken, Tony & Jane
Bennett, Bruce & Jill Beacham, Alan & Pat Cotton, Neil & Judith Constable, John
Early, Pat Findel-Hawkins, Tim & Lisa Parkinson, Charlotte & Steve Preston, Susie
Pitt, John George.

I would also like to thank all the many people with whom I worked at the mill
over the years, and who enjoyed it with me. Also, all the visitors who understood the
spirit of the place, and helped to build up its good feeling.

DESNA GREENHOW

Introduction

A WEEK BEFORE we were due to move into the Mill House the River Otter flooded the ground floor to a depth of two feet. Our son Denys would have liked the flood to be more dramatic than it was with the water coming up, if possible, to the first floor so that he could float his rubber dinghy out of his new bedroom window. As it was the incident was quite dramatic enough for me, completely ruining the decorations which had just been finished for our arrival.

This initiation gave us an idea of what the River Otter could do. Later we understood how we could help to divert floodwater away from our own and the other houses in the lower part of the village by operating the sluice gates which send water to and from the mill. But at that time we were novices. The derelict mill across the road was a closed book to us. I had no idea that one day I would be its miller, and that it would be working, and full of life once again.

We had come to live in Otterton when my husband Philip became assistant agent on the Clinton Estate. For several years we looked across the village street at the blank-faced building opposite and sometimes wondered about it. I knew that it was a watermill, or had once been, and that the occupants of our house had been millers, who had crossed the road to work every day until grinding had stopped about twenty years before. I did wonder about a small internal window in the house between the kitchen and the sitting room until an old lady living in a thatched cottage on the village green beckoned me over one day to tell me that a miller who had lived in our house a hundred years before had given the church clock to the village. I realised that you could see the clock from the kitchen through the little internal window and decided that the miller's wife must have said, 'if youm spendin all that money for the village, I want to be able to tell the time by that there clock any time I like.'

The children went to the village school just across the road and up the hill, and life was idyllic in many ways. We had a walled garden, completely neglected, but just waiting to be restored, and we had a happy time creating a lawn and borders and training fruit trees against the warm Tudor brick walls. I did a teacher's training, and found supply work in Otterton school, so the children and I crossed the road together in the mornings. Phil's job meant that we were accepted as part of the village (where the surnames had been the same since the middle ages, and in the sixties there were only three families of incomers). He was working with Devon farmers and craftsmen and had a position everyone understood in that part of the country.

After a time I became restless, however. I was not sure I wanted us to live on a rain-soaked flood plain forever, and began to get a feeling of wanting us to 'go where the action was' instead of settling for sleepy Devon.

In 1973 *Small is Beautiful* by E.F Schumacher was published. Reading press notices of the time, it is clear that many of our present doubts and fears were already outlined by Schumacher:

> . . . man's current pursuit of profit and progress, which promotes giant organizations and increased specialization, has in fact resulted in gross economic inefficiency, environmental pollution and inhumane working conditions. Dr.Schumacher . . . proposes a system of intermediate technology, based on smaller working units, communal ownership, and regional workplaces utilising local labour and resources.

At about the same time, I came across the philosopher Krishnamurthi. He wrote and taught a message that, simply put, said that we are far too busy trying to become something else, concentrating on the past and the future but not on the present, and that if we all did live in the present without trying endlessly to move on with our ambitions for the future the world would be in far greater harmony.

I realised that my children were growing up in the people-oriented small world which is a village, and that this was something precious and unique. Schumacher's ideas of small-scale, people-centred economics, and Krishna-murthi's advice to 'be', not to 'become', seemed good advice – to live the present with a hopeful heart and see what came in. Very soon after this an extraordinary opportunity came my way.

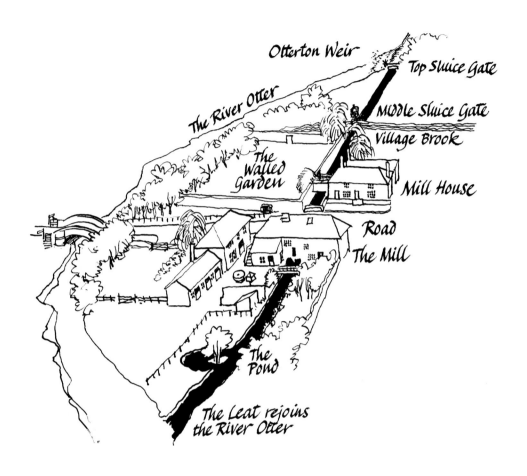

Otterton Weir

Top Sluice Gate

The River Otter

Middle Sluice Gate

Village Brook

The Walled Garden

Mill House

Road

The Mill

The Pond

The Leat rejoins the River Otter

Otterton Mill,
Otterton,
Budleigh Salterton,
Devon
EX9 7HG
tel: 01395-568521
email: escape@ottertonmill.com

Now bones lie in the yard
Reminder of the cattle days.
Here's the slaughterhouse,
Unwillingness and goaded fear still here.
Once waggons backed close to the loading bays.
The miller's pride and joy,
His horses, led out from the stable
Where turkeys perch and grow.

The mill itself.
We lift the noisy latch.
Beyond the door
The echoing sound of water.
Reflections catch the gears
And in the still, still building
The water races through
The place, asleep, waiting.

1
The Derelict Mill

'More water floweth through the mill
Than knows the miller of.' (ANON)

OTTERTON MILL is built in the local rough soft red sandstone which was quarried from shallow pits towards the cliffs in this part of East Devon to build simple local buildings such as barns, outhouses, and in this case a mill. It was considerably rebuilt from the first floor upwards in the mid-nineteenth century to judge by the brick window arches, but the tithe map of 1844 shows the same ground plan which is there today with the mill stream flowing through the centre of the mill to turn two mill wheels, side by side. The sandstone near ground level is worn and eroded and has clearly been there much longer than the upper part of the mill, while the front elevation is blank and it is impossible to see much of what is inside from the road.

When we were first in the Mill House the mill itself was leased to a grain haulier who used it as a store. He disliked the old machinery which he felt 'got in the way', and he sold off and sabotaged parts of it, and as a result he was unwilling to allow anyone inside the place who had anything to do with his landlords, the estate for which Phil was working. As you could not see through the grimy windows we had little idea about what was there.

The complex of out-buildings was leased separately to our local butcher, and until the fifties the large concrete yard to the west of the mill had been a cattle market. Though the market was closed down, the slaughterhouse was still in use and the old mill stables were used by Frank the butcher as his turkey rearing sheds. One Christmas, his turkeys were all stolen a day before they were due to be killed, and thirteen hundred of them were taken, packed into a lorry, and driven away in the middle of the night without any of us in the house hearing a thing! In about 1975 the grain haulier's lease was up and he left. Soon afterwards, Frank gave up the slaughterhouse and the turkey-rearing.

Discussions started in the estate office about what to do with the mill. The building surveyor found that it needed re-roofing whatever its future was to be. Later, I thanked him from the bottom of my heart for getting this done. If he had not it is likely that the mill would soon have been in a state of complete disrepair. At last there was a chance to see inside, and it was this initial visit which had such an impact on me that it made me determined to rescue the place.

M Y CHILDREN, Martha and Denys, and I entered from the road through the heavy stable door. The blacksmith-made latch and simple round handle (I later found that all the bolts, latches and handles were made by our local blacksmith) lifted noisily and once the door was open the sound of rushing water filled our ears. Inside to the right was one set of machinery, seen first as a complicated mixture of cog wheels and shafts, mainly made of wood, but with some metal parts as well. There was an impression of extreme antiquity and as if none of it could ever move again nor had moved for centuries. There were the signs of the grain haulier's activities. A large square hole about eight feet across had been roughly cut through to the floor above with a chain saw and acro-props were holding the building up. Turning away from this disturbing sight the two children and I went along the narrow passage to the right, from which the sound of falling water was booming out. The wheel chamber is a stunning sight. No-one, in all the years I have seen people coming on it for the first time, has failed to look impressed and astonished when they see it. Two great water wheels are lit by the reflections coming up from the mill stream glinting on their curved buckets, while the water rushes past and underneath them, making the whole space full of sound and movement. We were all round-eyed and silenced, and stood quietly, looking almost reverently at the sight. 'Come on, ' I said, 'let's see what's next. '

Carrying on through the mill we came to the second system of machinery. Since the mill has two wheels, each can turn two sets of stones, more than you would expect in a village cornmill. At least three sets of stones were being turned at the time of the Norman Conquest, I discovered, and then Otterton Mill was one of the largest in Devon. (See chapter 8, History of the Mill)

Up the steep staircase there were further scenes of dereliction. A pair of mill stones, four feet in diameter, and weighing, by the look of them, over two tons, seemed almost suspended in air. The boards beneath them had rotted and, once again, acro-props were holding them up. We tiptoed past, as the whole place was shaking a little. Through a door we came out into one of the most pleasing rooms I have ever seen. A long low space with only six feet of headroom in most parts was punctuated with wide windows letting in plenty of light. In the centre was an upright shaft carrying a lovingly made wooden gear wheel with cogs also of wood, and, in front of this an embedded mill stone had a rhyme on its surface. 'This stone worked the first time, March 28th, 1859'.

The children rushed to the windows. At the back the view was straight down the mill stream which flowed out of the centre of the building and turned a bend out of sight beyond chestnut trees.

It was disturbing to see how the place had been neglected and misused. Looking round, I could see down to the floor below through the eight foot hole and it seemed there had been a fire in the room not too long ago. A large piece of plastic sheeting had been nailed over charred joists and beams above us. Over the wheel chamber the floor was rotten and you could see down on to one of the wheels. In spite of the dereliction we all noticed the feeling of peacefulness there. There were a few reminders of a previous miller, – a cow horn nailed to the wall for him to hang his bailer twine on, and scribbled pricing for a delivery of flour. It felt as if the ghosts were friendly.

We climbed the ladder with its polished wooden stick of a handle to the top floor. A long cat walk ran the full length of the building with deep storage bins on either side crudely numbered with Roman numerals. 'Little rooms. ' said Martha. 'There ought to be a princess with a spinning wheel in one of them. ' They did look like secret rooms in a fairy story but small square holes in the floor of each showed where the grain used to be released down to the grinding stones below. We tiptoed along the catwalk. There were still sacks and dusty corn lying about and we looked round fearfully for signs of rats. However, they were long gone when the last corn was ground.

I BEGAN TO FEEL EXCITED. Here was a project which could meet my new-found ideas of what was important. To get this mill going again would be to see it working as a microcosm, – a tiny world of its own – but with a message which was far-reaching. It had been possible in the past to produce something valuable with a natural power source, not harming the environment in any way. Also, in one small system, quantities of flour could be produced and then turned into bread and cakes without any of the additives used in commercial production. It was something which perhaps I could make happen and which could involve some of my friends and neighbours in the village, and possibly benefit them.

I wanted to try out the idea on someone else to see if it was too wild to contemplate. My father seemed the obvious choice. He was in an interesting and not unrelated phase of his life. He had recently retired and had moved to Sidmouth, a few miles away. A doctor with a distinguished career behind him, he was deeply involved in setting up a centre of wide spiritual and philosophical search looking outside mainstream orthodox approaches to research in the sciences and medicine. He and his partners, one of whom had been Chief Scientist to the Ministry of Power, were also deeply concerned about the dangers of relying on non-renewable power sources. They founded what they named the Scientific and Medical Network. (This now has more than two thousand members world-wide.) Several maverick figures soon became involved including Schumacher. The group was interested in whatever ideas were a little wide of centre in researching scientific avenues. My father was an enthusiast with an infectious charm but a serious approach to matters he considered important, so our pub lunches near his new home became times of discussion about his project and mine, and he was excited about my dream of restoring a water mill to its original use, of producing flour by a natural power source harmless to the environment, and of showing people how the process was done, from beginning to end.

The practical drawbacks to making the dream a reality were easy to see. The place was in a very bad state. Outside there were grisly reminders of the slaughterhouse and bones and other debris littered the yard. The lovely stable was in the state you would expect after it had been used for many years for poultry rearing. The fittings of the slaughterhouse were still intact and out in the space which had been the cattle market part was a jungle of grass and weeds, part still had the metal bases of the cattle stands dotting its surface. Another important consideration was that there was very little money available. I had none of my own, my husband thought the whole idea mad, and my father, although very enthusiastic, was putting most of what he had into the centre he was involved in setting up with a friend in Sidmouth for complementary medicine and spiritual growth. Sadly, he was diagnosed in the winter of 1976 as having advanced cancer. This made me even more determined to turn the restoration of Otterton Mill into a reality so that he could see, I hoped, the fruits of our many hours discussing it while he was still well enough to enjoy life. He was a believer that anyone with what he thought a good idea should be encouraged to carry it through. I do not know if he ever thought I could succeed in getting the mill going again but he certainly gave me the moral support I so badly needed.

Unfortunately, he could not give time to becoming involved in a practical way with the mill restoration because of his other projects and his deteriorating health, and so I looked round to see if anyone else locally would like to take part. A local judge and his wife, George and Ida Polson, had recently rescued an interesting chapel nearby. I rang George and asked tentatively if he would like to become involved. He was enthusiastic, and jumped at the idea. We agreed that we would have to move fast to get planning permission in place and negotiations with the estate completed so as to try to open the mill again, partly restored, in the summer of 1977. It was enormously helpful to have George's support. He was a busy man working full-time in the Exeter courts, but he allocated what time he had to give where it would be most useful, in applying for planning permission, in helping publicize what we were doing, and in meeting any legal hiccups we might encounter.

I worked out a plan to show the estate. The beautiful first floor room would be an exhibition gallery. Some of the outbuildings would be used as craft workshops, and there would be a tea room. The most important part of the restoration would be getting the mill going again, to make flour by water power as it had done for nearly a thousand years.

The estate was sympathetic to the idea and was willing to grant us a licence for two years to see what we could achieve, provided the necessary negotiations were successful with the local authority. They offered George and me a loan to match what money we could put in. We each contributed £1, 000, and the estate lent us £2, 000. This was a start. It allowed us to go through the initial stages of putting in for planning permission, finding out about the drainage, and making a strategic and detailed plan of action. Permission was granted in April about three weeks before my father died. A brilliant clinician, he followed each stage of his illness with enormous courage. Many friends and admirers came to visit him while he was ill and he entertained them with his usual charm, warmth, and interest in their own problems. He cracked his last bottle of champagne a few days before he died and he and I talked through each step of our developing ideas daily until nearly the end. I had to bury my grief by throwing myself into the mill project wholeheartedly in the following frenetic months as I knew he would want me to. We aimed at an opening at the start of the summer holidays and fixed on July 26th, 1977.

EVERYTHING HAD TO BE DONE simultaneously and it is difficult to disentangle the time sequence that followed. Inside the mill the estate agreed to do some structural work to start us off. Enormous new beams, about 1 ft x 2 ft in diameter, and 10 ft long were swung into the wheel chamber from the stream and these strengthened the whole centre of the building. The floor boards removed on the first floor by the grain haulier were replaced. We decided that the floor over one of the wheels should be made of perspex so that you could see down into the wheel chamber from above. This increased the light down below as well. The shaky floor below one of the pairs of stones was repaired and the stones themselves, (weighing about three tons between them), were rolled out of the way on wooden rollers made from fencing posts in the same way heavy weights were moved around in antiquity. These were the main structural repairs and the estate made it clear they would take on no responsibility for anything more from then onwards. Restoring the machinery, bringing one of the wheels to life again, building casing round the stones, renewing parts which had rotted and fallen off, putting in new bearings, and if necessary, sluice gates, all these jobs were over to us. It was a daunting undertaking, and we were only able to complete part of it that summer. We were determined that the wheel and the machinery would at least be turning to show people how it worked.

By a stroke of luck Rex Wailes, a great expert on wind and water mills, was a cousin of Phil's mother. He was in his eighties, but agreed to come and do a survey of the mill machinery. He was an engineer, like many of the family, and we went round the mill with a tape recorder together while he gave a detailed run-down on its features. Ours is a breast shot wheel, which means that the water hits its curved buckets at waist level, and knocks them in a clockwise direction. The weight of the water is combined with a sideways thrust – more efficient than the old undershot wheel, where a few buckets catch what water they can as it flows by. The breast shot wheel was invented by a French engineer, M. Poncelet, in the eighteenth century, and was a precursor of the turbine. It is rare to find one in an English mill, it seems. Our wheels are cast-iron, made in Exeter in the early nineteenth century. Rex was interested in the mill stones, two of them being French burr stones made of a specially hard quartz quarried from the Paris basin. He told me that the rhymed dedications on them were unique.

T HE LOCAL PRESS had become interested and there was plenty of publicity. I had a call from a firm of mechanical engineers in Tiverton who had seen an article about the restoration in a local paper. They were responsible for maintenance in a textile factory dating from the nineteenth century, which until the second World War had used water power for some of its operations. The last millwright trained just before the war still worked for the firm and they wondered if we were looking for someone to restore the machinery. This was a piece of luck as the millwright's skill is very rare indeed. Rex told me not to allow anyone to touch the machinery except a trained millwright, not even an engineer, he said, because most of them are far too advanced in their thinking to be able to concentrate on something as simple as a water mill, part wood, part iron, which has reached its present state through constant weathering over many years. (It could be as disastrous as trying to straighten a wind-blown tree on a cliff edge, he added.)

Mr. Pook, the millwright from Tiverton, arrived and saw what needed to be done. He did not give the impression of being a hands-on engineer but he clearly understood what he was looking at. It was obvious that we could not get the system to the point of grinding flour that summer. There was just too much to do. He suggested that we get the wheel turning, in itself quite an undertaking, bedded down as it was on the stream bed with some of its buckets missing. As soon as it was turning, he explained, the gear wheels would turn too so any work that had to be done on them must be tackled at the same time. He was impressed that none of the great wooden gears needed renewing but the bearings on them were gone, as was all the softwood in the system. He thought it was realistic to think that the initial work could be done in a couple of months provided he could get a good enough pattern for the main bearing on the wheel shaft, which was badly damaged.

There were a myriad of other jobs to do in the following two and a half months. There was no fencing in place on the property, and planning permission was dependent on its being properly fenced, and a tarmac splay created to allow

better visibility for cars going in and out. Other essentials included a car park with firm standing, and trees to act as a softening screen as the mill is at the entrance to the village. Several old sheds were to be demolished. (I sold them to a local market gardener.) The whole place was badly in need of cleaning up and decorating, and most important, a lighting system must be installed instead of the odd lightbulb swinging at a dangerous height.

WE WANTED TO SET UP the exhibition gallery and the first exhibition was fixed for July to coincide with the opening of the whole complex. Access to the mill building was to be by a bridge across the stream still to be constructed, and my daughter Martha decided that the little space leading up to the door would be a Beatrix Potter garden. We had been given some suitable plants by my aunt, who had made just such a haven in the Lake District. We would have an English cottage garden with an emphasis on plants which butterflies and birds would enjoy such as sedums, buddleias, and plants for spreading scent in daytime and evening.

Soon there was a hive of activity in every part of the site. As one of the important parts of the plan was to involve as many people living in the village as possible we asked two retired estate employees who had worked in the forestry department and gardens for forty years and who lived in Otterton to do the fencing. They certainly enjoyed being involved, though the language that floated across the site was ripe when the bank of the mill stream gave way, and their new fence collapsed into the water – blame being shifted backwards and forwards between them for the rest of the afternoon.

Mike Earle, a builder based in the village, and an old friend, took on all the serious heavy work, the bridge, the landscaping, the splay to the road, the improvement of what was to be a ladies toilet, and the shelving and display spaces in the future craft shop. Friends both from the village and further afield volunteered to help Martha, Denys and me clear all the debris from the courtyard, the old cattle market and the future garden, including the grisly slaughterhouse waste. We found one or two treasures, including the metal sack stencils, inscribed with the words 'Otterton Mills'. In the past a sweep of a paint brush across them imprinted sacks of flour to show they had been ground at this particular mill.

We decorated the inside of the mill with masonry paint to give a brilliant white finish to the simple, rough stone walls. This had been done innumerable times in the past, but not for twenty years or so. The machinery was cleaned up and the different parts of the workings were labelled. Denys, who drew very well, made a wonderful relief map of the mill stream and the river and the mill premises between the two. We put in new circuits and carefully concealed light switches. Most of the lighting was by spotlights designed to put dramatic light on to the machinery and the wheels, and on to paintings and sculpture in the gallery, and to be as adaptable as possible.

Our budget was limited to say the least. For this initial stage we had our £4,000, and were relying on charging a small entrance fee, once we had anything to show, to pay for what we were doing. What seemed most important was that the mill should show itself off with as many of the signs of its original use as possible left just as they were. I had a strong feeling that this roughness, if it was contrasted with sparkling walls and good lighting would be the best way to show such a well-worn working environment. With that in mind we left the blacksmith-made nails which had once had a use and kept labelling down to a minimum. The mill is a Grade 2 star listed building and changes to it can only be minimal, but this fitted in with my determination not to turn it into a show case, as altering the interior could so easily lose the feel of it and chase the friendly ghosts of previous millers away! There was a strong responsibility not to take the restoration too far. I wanted it to be peaceful so that people could come and sit in the courtyard, perhaps with their bicycles propped against a mill stone, and the resident birds would not feel threatened, in fact the kind of place which is often bulldozed by progress.

It was essential to block out the reminders of the slaughterhouse and to improve the approach to the building as far as was possible given our strict budget. We did not want to lose the impact of the marvellous siting of the mill so we left the banks of the stream as they were, with no exotic planting. Lines from a poem by Gerard Manley Hopkins were constantly in my head:

> Where would the world be, once bereft
> Of wet and of wildness, let them be left.
> Oh, let them be left, wildness and wet.
> Long live the weeds and the wilderness yet.

We were leaving some places alone on purpose, but I felt we must contrast them with parts that we were making clean and tidy. It would be possible and easy for people to wander around, feeling that they are discovering the place for themselves on the way.

There was an office building which had been put up in the sixties, uninspiring to look at but structurally sound, and we decided to make this our tea room . A small part of it was partitioned off as a toilet and sink area and we turned this small space into a kitchen. We would offer cream teas and home-made cakes seven days a week.

A couple, Mona and Frank, who had recently retired from running one of the local pubs, came to work full-time, and all of us who had baking skills made the cakes and scones. The recipes were based on my home baking for the family, with help from my mother-in-law, who was an inspired tea time baker. Several people living in the village worked part time and very soon the café was staffed.

Here was another place which needed decorating, and a group of us turned our hands to this. We kept it simple with no frills. There are some wonderful river walks on the doorstep, and I wanted people to feel at ease when they entered in their walking boots. Our welcome, we hoped, combined with the freshly cooked cakes and scones, would set the mood. 'Oh, no, ' I said, we won't have tea bags. Only loose leaf tea. ' On the first day we opened, a very polite couple called over the first brand-new waitress. 'Excuse me, but we haven't got any tea bags in this pot. ' 'We don't use tea bags', said my friend, proudly. 'But, there isn't any *tea* in the pot', they explained. There is a strong empathy in this country with simplicity, and ironically enough, it becomes harder and harder to find, though I agree, you should be offered tea in your tea pot!

I WAS DREADING supervising the creation of the car park. Nothing in my experience had taught me how many tons of hardcore you need to create a car park for fifteen cars. Mike Earle would not have time to make the car park as well as finish the work he was doing already and in any case, we could not afford to give him the job. Luckily, a large area in Exmouth was being bulldozed to make a new complex round the docks. Would we need ten tons of rubble, or two hundred ? If I got it wrong we would be digging too deeply into our limited money supply. The only alternative was to decide, when each load arrived and was rolled flat, how much more it looked as though we still needed. It was not the easiest way for the hauliers to work but they were very patient and kind and in a week we had half a car park, finished neatly with chippings. The other half is on hard standing where the cattle market once was and we decided not to alter it. Soon about twenty five cars could be fitted in. I was very relieved when that part of my responsibility was over.

TIME WAS MOVING ON. Mr Pook the millwright had taken away a twisted bearing from the water wheel and had measured the curved buckets or blades, some of which he was replacing to allow the wheel to turn evenly and efficiently. Three weeks went by with no word from him. We had a month left before the opening and it seemed impossible that everything would be done in time.

Mike and his team finished the outside work, and at last the bridge was in place and the path up to the door. I was relieved, as until then it had been difficult to landscape the little garden. John, a sensitive gardener who had worked in my father's community in Sidmouth and was interested the healing aspects of plants, worked with Martha, and between them they began to create a magic space. The garden slopes down sharply to the stream, and the brick path the builders created curves through it, leaving flower beds on each side with interesting combinations of textures and colours, created by Martha, who was very clever at achieving unusual effects with plants. She carried on using these skills in other parts of the complex over the following years.

At last I managed to get hold of Mr Pook. He had had great difficulty in creating a pattern for the new bearings. Even with his precision engineering skills he had had to make a prototype in resin for the foundry to work to. The bearing would have to carry the iron wheel, weighing about four tons. It was three metres in diameter, and about a metre wide. When it was turning at its maximum speed the stress on the bearings would be considerable. Mr Pook anticipated that he would be at the mill to fit bearings and buckets in the second week of July. This would only be a few days before the opening and I wondered how my nerves would stand it. The whole thing felt like a roller coaster ride, but a very exciting one. The enthusiasm of everyone working on the project buoyed me up, and the adrenalin rush was renewed every day.

S EVERAL ARTISTS showed work in the first exhibition. My friends Brenda Carter, a still life painter and her husband Ken, a sculptor, and the painter Alan Cotton, and his wife, Pat, helped get the gallery ready, as did the children. We all painted the walls, and scrubbed down the ancient wooden beams, joists and floors. We sent out invitations to the opening and a poster, the first of many, was designed and printed.

An amateur film-maker in the village made a video of the restoration. It has background music which gathers pace as D- day approaches. I was asked to put a commentary to it 'live', without having seen it first, not the easiest of briefs, and synchronicity leaves a great deal to be desired. At one point I say, 'There were some important jobs left to be done,' and we switch to Denys and a friend, aged thirteen, enthusiastically painting the chicken house door. The film, however, is in other ways a valuable record of those hectic months.

Three days before the opening, Mr Pook and his men arrived with the bearings and buckets and a hoist to lift the wheel off the stream bed. They worked unbelievably quickly and soon the buckets were in place, the wheel lifted and lowered on to the new bearings, which were greased ready for the moment of truth. A radio journalist was interviewing me just as Mr Pook went up the orchard to the top sluice gate to let some water through from the river. The recording contains the sound of the sudden rush of water to the wheel while I, extremely excited, exclaim loudly, 'Now the wheel is actually turning, it's really turning, the first time for twenty years. '

THE BUILDERS DECIDED to create a fitting use for some old mill stones which were propped up in the car park. First they built three strong brick plinths in the courtyard, ready to support the one and a half ton stones. Then they made use of a small crane to lift each stone, bring it into the yard, and lower it on to a plinth, making a table. Very skilled work, as the stone swung about dangerously, and had to be placed very exactly in position. Also, a kindly gesture towards the grand opening.

This was a great success. The archive film shows about a hundred people exploring the mill, wine glasses in their hands, enjoying the exhibition, doing their best not to bang their heads on the low beams, and listening to speeches, Judge Polson's being the star turn. We none of us realized that ten weeks later George Polson would be dead after a by-pass operation, and the full weight of the project would be on my shoulders. More than once I felt I really was carrying one of those stones round my neck.

The following winter without my father's and George's support I also felt I was wading through treacle and that I would never be clear of it, but as things turned out the following years were probably the most interesting of my life.

I HAVE DECIDED not to tell the story of the mill project chronologically, but to base the memories, poems and facts about milling, on each part of the mill itself. Perhaps it will seem like an unfolding screen, each panel showing up the wheel, or the stream or the other parts of the place, a kind of testament to twenty-five years of varied activities and impressions, with the down-to-earth background of what happens in a working water mill to give it a solid base.

Tumbling down the Blackdown hills
A stream, not seeing its destination,
Known by the trout who make it up that far,
To spawn beneath the overhangs
In cooling, calming eddies.
Known by dragonflies, and enterprising herons,
Choosing to fish where there is no disturbance.
Known by the kingfishers and dippers,
With little need to keep their nestlings hidden.
Down, down it comes, part of it caught
Into a narrow, boarded flow,
Diverted centuries ago.
And here its business crosses ours
Turning our wheels before it hits the sea.

2
The Mill Stream

WHEN WE FIRST CAME to live in the Mill House we could hardly get up to the top of the orchard, it was so overgrown. The magnificent head weir is about sixty feet wide, a beauty spot reached from the other side of the river from the mill property. The mill stream runs down one side of the orchard, the river down the other, and the village brook and the overflow from the stream tumble across the end over rocks which form good fishing grounds for dippers. So the orchard is an island, which had been undisturbed for quite some years when we came on the scene.

The mill stream follows a good, straight line. The sandstone cliffs above the weir shoot water into the narrow channel controlled by sluice gates, which can send a maximum amount of water through the mill for grinding, or can be diverted back to the river when the flow is not needed, to save the erosion of the banks. The stream as it leaves the river runs for a short way beside a steep wooded bank covered in spring with snowdrops, which must have been there from time immemorial. Then it opens out and runs beside gardens and the orchard. After snow one year we saw a fox's footprints where it had crossed the sluice gate along the metal top which is only two inches wide.

This is the lowest point in the Otter where a water mill could have been built, but this river is difficult to direct, being wide and shallow, and once it ended in an estuary at Otterton. To serve the mill, a leat or stream was dug in the middle ages, and a weir built to divert the meandering river and give a good straight rush of water to turn the new mill wheels.

T HE FIRST SUMMER we were there, we cut a path through to the head weir using machetes and hooks of various kinds, disturbing the butterflies, which had had the place to themselves for many years. It was that summer too that otters used the holt beside the top pool. They were not deterred by us, and brought up their young in the long dark hole which went back into the cliff behind the sandy shore of the pool. This was the last time we saw them there. The late sixties saw a steep decline in the otter population on the river of its name, as in so many others. Once many years later, camping beside the pool, I heard the splash of a large animal diving into the water in the middle of the night, too large to be a mink. Since the late nineties there have been many more sightings, and otters have bred a few miles further up the river in a stretch less frequented by dogs.

The pool below the top sluice gate is three or four feet deep and I used to think of it as my jacuzzi. The children learned to swim there in hot summers, and I would lie on my back and be gently washed downstream a little way until my shoulders came up against a ridge of sand. Several times, kingfishers flew above us without having realized we were there, then uttered their shrill angry cries at having their space invaded. Once I was drying off on the bank, and my daughter, Martha was snorkelling below in the pool. I could see that at any moment she would catch sight of a large eel ahead of her. When she did, there was a moment of horrified realization, and then she erupted from the pool like an emerging sea monster, probably scaring the eel as much as it had frightened her.

The small stretch of the river which is diverted into this man-made stream has reached a swift pace sited, as it is, in the valley bottom. The Otter is only twenty-six miles long, rising in the Blackdown hills and taking a steep course in its higher reaches, so different and secret compared with its wide, meandering progress here near the mouth. One day, lying in the pool, I found myself wondering about life in the upstream stretches, and wrote the poem at the beginning of this chapter as I was washed gently against my sand bar, and then swam a few strokes up to the sluice gate again and again.

T RADITIONALLY, MILL STREAMS are lined with elm boarding, the wood which lasts best under water. Dutch elm disease and the neglect which comes with so many water mills having become non-viable, mean that lining a mill stream has become too much of a luxury to be contemplated. However, the banks and bed have to be cleared of weed and the silt which has been washed down, and some lining of the sides is necessary to keep the banks from becoming eroded. My husband, Phil, took very seriously the task of keeping the mill stream clear and running freely, and of altering the sluice gates so that we could protect the lower part of the village and, of course, the Mill House from flooding.

There are various circumstances which can produce flooding in Otterton. Torrential rain upstream can make the river rise suddenly as much as seven or eight feet in a few hours. Then, the head weir turns into a horizontal, raging monster, taking everything in its path. The water meadows are usually flooded and often the road out of the village is impassable. The meadows below the mill become covered with river silt. The top sluice gate at the entrance to the stream has so far always just held back the torrent but with the water sometimes only a few inches from spilling over the top, I always felt that if it did come over, it would flood the houses near river level quite easily. On the village green there is a granite standing stone pointed out to me in the early days by an old lady as 'very ancient'. Looking closely at it I found nicks cut in it a foot apart up to four feet, and it was clearly put there to measure flood levels some time in the past. The water meadows act as a failsafe device to take most of the flood water away from the village when there is a sudden rise in the river level, but the situation can be complicated by spring tides, as we are only about a mile inland. If there is a flood at high tide the water in the mill stream is sometimes stationary as tide meets river, and then decisions have to be made as to how to turn the sluice gates so as to send as much water as possible back to the river.

Flooding can come from another direction when surface water tumbles down the surrounding hills and feeds into the village brook. The small bridges which cross the brook to access the houses along the street sometimes become blocked and then quite exciting results can follow. Once on my birthday, which is near Christmas, there was a sudden downpour while Martha, a friend, and I were discussing where we would go for a meal. We were astonished to look out of the front door, and see a torrent running down the street. I had my leg in plaster and a new carpet was rolled up on the dining-room floor ready to be laid the following morning. 'Oh, what about the crafts in the shop in the mill?' said the girls, and they started across the road to lift everything up out of the way of the flood. I looked helplessly out of the window to see them reach the other side as cars and masonry began to be washed past the house. Phil fortified the small wall outside the house and the front door with flood boards, sandbags, and anything he could lay his hands on, to save the house from flooding. Several neighbours who were away had water rushing in at their front doors and out at the back. As usual, the flood subsided as quickly as it had started, and thank heavens, the girls got safely back, having saved some valuable crafts in the shop from being ruined.

EVERY SUMMER we had to shut the sluice gates down completely and stop the flow so that we could clear weed from the stream bed to keep a good strong flow to the mill. In the early days Harry, a Devonian who had lived in the area all his life, did this clearing with great thoroughness and continued well into his eighties. He donated an invaluable and ancient curved fork to us for hooking weed and clearing gratings. The heavy wodges of weed have to be cut well back and lifted on to the bank where they are left for several days so that insects, and even small fish fry can wriggle back into the water. As the mill stream is about half a mile long, this clearing takes some time. The children used to enjoy taking buckets and rescuing eels, trout and sea trout living in the deeper pools under the alder and willow trees along the banks.

According to a medieval record the annual clearing of the mill stream was one of the feudal dues of the men of Yettington, a small hamlet half a mile from Otterton. I have often wondered how their clearing party compared with ours, or did one man volunteer? – perhaps an ancestor of Harry's, given that until the last twenty years there was very little movement out of or into the village, and the same names appear in the records as far back as the fourteenth century.

Once the mill was operating again and when Harry had retired, each summer a different team of strong young men and women working at the mill in the café or bakery had a few days in the open air in their wet suits, waders, or bare-legged in trainers, to do this work. Once, a powerful rugby player named Darren pulled out what he thought was an old car tyre. It turned out to be a very indignant eel who had clearly lived there for a long time and grown to an enormous size. Darren looked as if he would have much preferred to be in a rugby scrum than face it!

W E DID NOT CLOSE the top sluice gate completely except when absolutely necessary, so that the resident fish would not be starved of oxygen. By improving the flow and keeping it clear of weed, the stream gradually became an essential stretch for brown trout and sea trout to spawn in during the winter months. Until a fish pass was built recently to allow fish to get up the weir they could not follow their instincts to breed higher up the river, and some settled for the quiet reaches of the mill stream, choosing the gravel stream bed near the house to lay their eggs, where they were fairly safe from herons. To begin with we could not understand what the noisy splashings were on clear nights in October and November. Soon though, we were able to see the fish about their business. The female spends some time making a hollow in the gravel with her tail, and by rolling the whole of her body on one side. When she is satisfied that the hole she has made is deep enough, she starts to lay her eggs, again with splashings and heavings. Seen from our kitchen window, above the scene, the male, which is often smaller than her, seems to be hovering anxiously for some time, but then, eventually, deposits his sperm. The indentations the fish make are called redds. The fertilized eggs are vulnerable and may be washed away in floods or eaten by ducks or geese. It is not unknown for a heron to go for the spawning fish while they are distracted, though it is difficult for such a large bird, with its great wing-span, to rise from such a narrow space as the mill stream, where it flows between the house and the wall of the garden. It disappears under the road, and then flows through the mill. The sound of the water wheel turning echoes back. So if you forget to turn the sluice gates down in the evening, you are reminded by the noise.

The wheel is hidden from outside, being in the centre of the mill, and the stream rattles under loose boards inside the building before it turns them.

(These boards must be kept moveable, so that they can be lifted, and debris cleared from the sluice gates which control the wheel.) There is a drop of about four feet inside the wheel chamber, and only a couple of inches clearance between the wheel and the stone floor, so the clearing of this debris is important. The wheel has often jammed through something as small as a stick being caught under it. Upstream there are two gratings to catch any logs, leaves, or loose weed before they reach the mill, and these we always kept clear, using Harry's invaluable and ancient curved fork.

T HE FIRST WINTER we were at the Mill House, the hounds were still legally hunting otters. Soon after there was a ban, to everyone's relief, as the numbers of otters had dropped so drastically. The hunts are still allowed to chase mink, and there are quite a few of these fierce little animals on the Otter. Mink kill for fun, ducks, hens, fish, and even, once, I have seen one kill a goose. One of our geese was sailing tranquilly along on the river, when it started to subside, front forward, into the water. It was being pulled down by a mink, and seemed too astonished to realize what was happening. I splashed into the river, shouting angrily at the mink to let go but the goose was so badly injured, and in such a state of shock, that it died soon afterwards.

There was a debate for many years as to whether it was the increase of the mink population which led to the decline of otters, but conservationists have decided that lack of deep water pools, pollution which affects otters badly as they are at the top of the food chain, and disturbance by dogs on the river banks and in the water are to blame. Sadly, a few miles upstream from the mill, a female otter which was suckling her young was found shot a year or two ago. The pups were never discovered, but must have died of starvation. Not everyone in the countryside is friendly to the otter.

One busy day at the mill the hounds were hunting mink on our stretch of the river. The mill courtyard was full of people and a group was standing on the little footbridge, pointing excitedly into the stream. A Laocoan struggle was going on between a mink and a large eel. They were rolling over and over, the mink trying to catch the eel by the throat, and they were being washed downstream, too absorbed in the struggle to swim against the flow. Another mink was swimming in the same pool, perhaps encouraging his friend. I was amused by the idea that perhaps all the mink in the area had gravitated to the safety of the mill, knowing that the hounds could not follow them there. I hurried off to the road bridge over the river to see what the hounds were up to. All the old men of the village were there, and comments were flying around as to the likelihood of them catching a mink. 'Ooh, no, them won't catch anything. Not a chance. ' They were gleeful at the thought of the mink hiding at the mill. I suddenly noticed that some of the hounds had crossed the river and were in our orchard, in which we had several beehives. There was a hiatus, it seemed, with the huntsman unable to get them back. I rushed into the orchard, and found some frantic hounds, shaking bees out of their coats, and rubbing them off their faces. No hope of catching anything that day.

The mink which live in the mill stream can be a real nuisance, however. One night I lost forty-one of our forty-two hens when one got into the chicken house. Most were simply killed, not eaten. Mink are fearless, too, and once a visitor saw a hen disappearing backwards under the hen house in an unnatural way. He tried to pull it out but there was a mink attached to the other end of it which would not let go. He did win the battle in the end, but the hen was too badly hurt to recover. One year when a water bailiff still patrolled the river he caught seventeen in our half mile stretch, and the following year there were just as many about. The males take over any vacated stretch of river and move in their harems. They breed every few months so there is not much hope of controlling their numbers.

E VEN BEFORE THE RESTORATION of the mill, this part of the river bank was a favourite walk, and crowded with walkers at weekends. Every kind of walk is available, from the stroll up to the weir, to the ten mile round, and there is the opportunity to walk the East Devon Way, which is thirty-seven miles long, or the coastal path, about the same length. The footpath follows the river bank on the far side from our orchard. Walking through the orchard with liberal-minded friends first gave me the idea of sharing our enormous piece of luck at living in such a beautiful place. I was pointing out how we were on an island, the orchard being surrounded by water. Our friend Anthony said quietly, 'Yes, I expect a lot of people would like to share this with you. ' As things developed, the orchard itself remained far more private than the rest of the property. It was a haven to retreat to when there were as many as seventy thousand people a year coming to the mill across the road. Anthony's remark, however, stayed with me, and sowed a seed about sharing some of this magic place with other people.

The head weir at the top of the mill stream is the most recent version, superseding many others which were probably washed away by floods over the centuries. This one did not allow migratory fish to swim upstream to spawn although in the autumn many tried, throwing themselves against the concrete walls of the weir, and swimming frantically upwards until they fell back, exhausted, before they reached the top lip. Only when the river was high enough to create an oxygenating froth of water at the bottom of the weir but not so high as to make it impossible for fish to fight against its flow did a few make it upstream. Even then they had to contend with the herons who sometimes seemed so full of fish they found it difficult to fly.

A scheme was floated to build a fish pass. I was worried to begin with that the free-flowing water down the pass would affect the amount of water entering the millstream and thus the power to the wheel. The necessary finance was gathered together including a large contribution from Tesco's, and the work began. The foreman understood my anxieties. While the work was in progress we had to divert as much water as possible through the mill in order to do some necessary repairs, and the weir pool had to be emptied. This extra flow increased the erosion of the stream banks and actually broke one of the sluice gates inside the mill. Thoughtfully, the foreman changed the strategy so that some of the water was pumped downstream, and a small dam was built. As the water drained away, Environment Agency men in wetsuits with large nets and dustbins rescued the fish from the pool, took them up above the weir and released them. The fishermen had always maintained that there were hardly any sea trout in that pool. In the event it turned out that there were more than a hundred! It was an awesome sight to see quite large fish being lifted in the nets, weighing as much as eight pounds. I stood on the promontory at the top of the orchard, and photographed the scene. It was extraordinary to see the large pool, so much a part of our lives, completely empty and devoid of life. You could see the remains of previous weirs, some wooden-built, some with large granite columns, now lying randomly on the ground. The present weir had been eroded back beneath its base, making a cavern in which the fishermen conjectured most of those hundred sea trout had been hiding. Only four salmon were found in the pool, but we were all glad there were any because the salmon stocks in the Otter were said to be practically down to nil.

A lease for the mill of 1814 heavily protects the salmon rights of the landlord, Lord Rolle. A salmon hutch had been built in the lower reaches of the stream, and a weir constructed where the stream rejoined the river, to divert the migrating salmon up to the hutch. This was a trap which left the fish high and dry on a slab let into the side of the stream. The lease threatens the tenant miller with a fine if he is found to be poaching his lordship's salmon. An affidavit of 1853 making an application to introduce a policeman to Otterton has a low opinion of the inhabitants of the village in regard to this salmon hutch, as well.

> A large proportion of the inhabitants bear a bad character many of them appearing to live well without any visible means, . . . depredations are almost a constant occurrence also plunder by night and malicious injury to property, such as breaking down gates and carrying off railings, lopping trees for firewood and robbing gardens. . . . the salmon hutch belonging to the estate situated in the mill leat just below the village has been broken open once in the season for many years past and all the fish stolen.

Salmon poaching by millers seems to have continued, however. The outside lavatory was sited above the mill pool, and attracted plenty of fish to the spot. Millers are said to have sat there reflectively, pulling in good catches on a daily basis!

When the fish pass was being built my friend the foreman solved the problem of some of the water flow to the mill being lost by installing a row of concrete blocks a short way along the top lip of the weir. These help to carry the river flow in the direction for which this and all previous weirs were built, diverting water along the mill stream, to power the wheels. The pass has been a success, and sea trout have been able to spawn some miles upstream since 2002.

Whereas a wallow in the mill stream was refreshing on a hot day, the river above the weir is over six feet deep, and it is possible to dive, and swim some way. I liked resting my arms on the top of the weir, and looking down its full depth, on eye level with any mallards which happened to be grazing on its surface, seeing the sun sparkling on the water below. My aunt had what she said was her last swim in this pool, when she was well into her eighties, accompanied by neices, grandchildren and great grandchildren, on a lovely day in August, with water boatmen scudding away over the surface, disturbed by the shouts of the children sliding down the weir.

W E TOOK EVEN GREATER CARE to keep the water of the stream flowing well when, two years after the initial opening, we were ready to start grinding again. Mr Pook, the millwright who had done the work on the wheel two years before, came back to quote for the next phase. The fact that we had a good flow and had maintained the stream, not allowing it to silt up, which can be the death blow to many such projects, was crucial, since it is the force of the water under the wheel, as opposed to its depth, which builds up the power to turn the stones.

I had to think very hard as to whether we could afford to take the restoration through to its logical conclusion and make flour. We were still very short of money and had relied on the initial injection of capital, and the revenue from visitors, to keep the place going. (In all, capital investment was £14, 000 over the twenty-five years I was there). If we could not carry it through it seemed that the whole project might turn out to be meaningless in the terms in which I had envisaged it. However I did eventually decide to take the plunge and go ahead.

Mr Pook built new casing round the stones, made sure the water flow was strong enough to turn the wheel, and renewed the bearings on the gear wheels;

and then, I assumed, we would be off, milling regularly. I overlooked the fact that my knowledge of the art was very limited, and that as you are dealing with a natural power source, you are at the mercy of the weather and your own inexperience.

Mr Pook's work on the machinery did lead to my starting my career as a miller, however. The delicate interaction between the force of the water, the amount of grain being fed into the stones, and the distance between them is a constantly fascinating calculation, done by rule of thumb, according to how much it has rained, how much moisture there is in the air, how clear the mill stream is, and how well maintained the parts of the machinery are. Each time you want to start up, you look first at the state of the stream, and you clear debris from the gratings. Regularly you need to sluice the stream through, by opening the middle sluice gates, and raising the top one, so that silt is washed away back to the river. The water level rises significantly, and it is essential that it is diverted away from the wheel, which could be badly damaged by too much water suddenly being forced under it. There is always a danger in its being allowed to freewheel. The machinery then goes round too fast, and as it is delicate, almost certainly it will end up slightly out of true. Sometimes a long time has to be spent in getting it into good heart again. We always kept a padlock on the top sluice gate so that anyone crossing the weir, and seeing an interesting looking handle, could not turn it. Altering the water level, up or down, has consequences inside the mill which anyone half a mile upstream would be unaware of.

Next, you lower the top sluice gate again so that there is only a gap of about six inches at its base. This is quite enough water with the good flow we have to turn the wheel at most times of year. In the summer holidays, when the population is swelled by visitors, more water is taken from the boreholes to supply extra needs, and at the same time, the river is low, so that a little more water is needed to make milling possible. Even then, I could often only make perhaps, forty pounds or so of flour in a day, compared with the same amount in half an hour when conditions were at their best.

Having worked to achieve the correct flow to the mill, you put the machinery in gear, and then close the two sluice gates inside the mill, which have been diverting water away from the wheel. Now, there is a build-up of water behind the gate which controls the wheel. You do not open that until the stream is nearly at the top of it so that there is a rush of water to start a good momentum going.

The difficult times are when the stream is sluggish. Apart from the low flow in the summer, there is the autumn leaf and apple fall, which clogs the gratings as soon as you have cleared them, and the late spring/early summer weed growth which can slow the flow considerably.

MANY CIRCUMSTANCES make milling impossible from time to time. When the water is too high a backward thrust counteracts the force and makes the wheel turn slowly. In any case, a high water level implies that there will almost certainly be debris which can jam it. This may sometimes be freed by strong people, (I have to be sexist here) usually men, who can put their weight against the wheel, and turn it slightly in an anti-clockwise direction, thus freeing whatever has made the jam. A more serious blockage needs a slight lifting of the wheel with a jack. For most of the time I was at the mill, I had expert help and support from the estate's team who normally dealt with problems in their farm machinery. They were able to build new sluice gates when we needed them, and to clear the wheel when it jammed. This only happened three or four times in twenty-five years.

Milling is impossible when there is a hard freeze-up. We had one particularly exciting experience of this in the early nineties. On a very cold morning Phil had not yet gone to work, when we realized that a great deal of water was coming down the mill stream. Up at the top of the orchard we saw that the weir was frozen over, which meant that the whole of the river was being channelled down the stream. We saw that the middle sluice gate was frozen solid, with such a build-up of ice that the water could not get away down to the river. We roped ourselves so as not to get swept away, as the concrete floor was like glass, and let ourselves down cautiously with crowbars to try to clear the ice. Everything metal was so cold that the crowbars stuck to hands or gloves. However, we managed to create a channel for some of the water to escape. Worse faced us inside the mill, where the wheel chamber had turned into an ice cavern, beautiful but dangerous, because to free the water there you were in danger of slipping down several feet under the disused wheel. So, for several hours we worked on it, until at last we could move the gates again. People in the lower village never knew they were saved from what would have been quite a flood, with the whole river behind it. When people asked me if we had had problems during the freeze-up, I took a deep breath, and did not always tell the story, which sounded too dramatic to be true. At the time, though, it felt as if we were in a Victorian novel, perhaps *The Mill on the Floss*, and that we would inevitably be swept away. As Mr Tulliver says to his son Tom in George Eliot's novel, 'Water is not like hay, Tom. You can't lift it with a pitchfork. '

A s TIME WENT ON, the stream became an important part of people's enjoyment in visits to the mill. Our small footbridge, only four feet wide, became a favourite place for poohsticks. Hours were spent watching eels, or Tommy the trout, who was fed by our chef, Susie, until he grew to an enormous size and could hardly hide under the rocks. In the early days thousands of elvers came up the stream in spring, but no more. Only the adult eels are left.

Our cat, appropriately named Milly, was the only cat I ever knew who could catch eels. She would sit for hours with her face close to the water, I suppose a strange, whiskery shape on the surface to the eel she had her eye on. Eventually it would swim up to see what this strange thing was, and she would grab it with one swift paw, and soon be eating it noisily, bones and all.

Once we had a Puppet Festival at the mill, with five Puppet companies taking part. As a finale, we had a day of workshops, where children made puppets representing all the animals round the mill in preparation for the surprise of the afternoon. We had mice, fish, spiders, doves, hens and eels. Jane Paterson, the lovely puppeteer who co-ordinated the day, told the children a story of how there was a wicked dragon who drank up all the water in the mill stream, so that the mill would not work, and all the animals were getting thirsty, as well. What was needed was for all the children and their animal puppets to make as much noise as possible to frighten the dragon away. They had all brought saucepans, and drums, and other things to make as much noise as possible. I closed down the sluice gates, so that there was no water coming through the stream, and then, in the twilight, an enormous dragon came across the bridge to where the children were gathered in the courtyard. We all made a great deal of noise, and the dragon sank down, and staggered away. I let the water through again with a rush. We all clapped and felt happy. Those clever puppeteers had made the dragon for a street carnival, and with five of them inside it, it looked very menacing. We were glad we had outwitted it!

Twisted metal buckets turn their lumbering cycle
Again, endlessly, until I change the sluices,
Stop the flow, and cut it dead. Then the wheel,
Obedient to my hands, stops instantly, leaves dripping
    water
On its glittering blades. The wheel chamber is silent.
Can it really be that moments since
That great creature turned on its axle?
Has it ever? It sits, immovable, ancient-seeming.
Reflections show the water racing past.
Impossible to believe it turns gears, stones,
Makes flour appear, as if by magic.

3
The Mill Wheel

I F A PLACE has a heart, the heart of this mill is in the wheel chamber. Two great dripping water wheels are lit at different times of day in different kinds of weather by the reflections coming up from the mill stream, glinting on the surface of the one we use, and casting shadows on the wall in the case of the one we don't use. It is a magic cavern when the sun is shining, a sinister and powerful cave when it is not.

The Romans used water wheels, but did not develop their technology very extensively, probably because there was a slave economy in most of the Empire. When Christianity came to Western Europe, labour was regarded as essential to carry out God's work, but labour-saving devices were, all the same, well worth developing when you had to carry out that work yourself. It was in the monasteries, where manual work counted for so much, that the early water mills were to be found. At the Norman Conquest there were over five thousand of them in England, developed by the Saxons, in a quiet technological revolution which went largely unrecorded.

In steep mountainous regions a horizontal wheel was fixed over a stream, and the rushing water turned it. It was attached to a simple gearing system, at the end of which a pair of stones revolved. This method is still used in a few mills in the north of Scotland and in mountains in other parts of the world. (I came on a horizontally driven corn mill in Nepal worked by a woman, who only invited the women in our party to come inside and see what she was doing. Unfortunately language difficulties made it impossible for me to tell her that I, too, was a 'lady miller', or 'milleress'!) More common than the horizontal wheel is the vertical one. Early on this was simply placed in a river or stream, so that water was caught by the few paddles or buckets which touched the surface as the flow passed them. This was known as an 'undershot' wheel. A big improvement came when it was realized that more power could be generated if the water came over the top of a wheel and pushed it round from above. A stream powered in this way has to be diverted through a channel, usually made of wood, named a 'launder'. It is the most common kind of water wheel still in use in this country, and is known as an 'overshot' wheel. The one in our mill, which is known as 'breastshot', is less common. Here the water hits the wheel at waist level, and turns it clockwise, with a combination of sideways thrust, and weight on the curved buckets. This system is a forerunner of the turbine. As I discovered soon after starting milling it works more efficiently if you open the sluice gate behind it only slightly and allow a jet of water to turn it, rather than opening the sluice gate wide and following your instinct to get as much water as possible on to the buckets.

In Otterton at the time of the Norman Conquest there was enough power to turn three sets of stones, which implies that there were two water wheels, even then. This was already an important manor, owned by the mother of King Harold, who was killed by William of Normandy at the battle of Hastings in 1066. (see chapter 8 for the history of the mill).

W HEN MY CHILDREN AND I first went inside the mill and saw the two wheels, lying, probably, in the same position as the original ones, it did look unlikely that it would be possible ever to get either of them moving again. The one on the left of the chamber still has its ruined wooden buckets. The horizontal shaft that connects it to the gears consists of a trunk of a large oak tree about two foot in diameter, sitting on plain bearings made of iron. The oak shaft was not in a state to be rescued, and the idea of replacing it by another of the same size would be an enormously expensive undertaking. I discovered from Rex Wailes, who did the survey of the machinery, that the two wheels were twins, made in Exeter in the early nineteenth century, of cast iron. They both would originally have had wooden buckets. They were both settled down firmly into the bed of the stream.

The buckets on the right-hand wheel had been replaced by metal ones, probably in the time of the one miller, John Uglow, who made improvements to the workings, in the late eighteen fifties. (See chapter 8). That was a time when the survival of small stone-grinding water wheels was in jeopardy, because of the use of turbines, and the development of roller mills, which could turn out a far greater volume of flour than was possible from a wheel-driven system, depending, as it does, on the vagaries of the weather and the seasons.

THERE IS A DANGEROUS SITUATION when milling is going on, if the wheat is not fed steadily down into the stones. The cushion of grain between them acts as a brake on the speed of the wheel's turning. One of the pleasures in milling is to judge that you have the right distance between the stones to give them an optimum chance of grinding grain into flour of the fineness that you want. If the feed is not constant, the braking action does not work, the water wheel begins to spin out of control at great speed, the stones heat up dangerously, and the gears and bearings easily become damaged, unnerving for anyone without experience, as I was.

In 1979, on the first day I started milling again, Bert Rawlings, who had been miller at Otterton for many years, and Norman Buckle, who ground barley for animal feed for the last three years before its closure in 1959, were with me. They both brought their grandchildren to see where the grandfathers had worked. The place was full of people, as there had been plenty of publicity about milling starting again. I was feeling very nervous, and was trying to give the impression I was confident, which was far from being the case. Suddenly, the wheel started to turn wildly. Clearly, the grain was not feeding into the stones properly. All three of us, Bert, Norman and I raced upstairs to open wider the flap which controls the trickle of grain. There had probably never before been three millers in the mill at the same time, dealing with a problem only they had any clue about, even if one of them, me, only had a dim idea of what to do. They filled me in, of course, in a lesson I never forgot.

Bert Rawlings was a broad, powerful man, the picture of a miller, with a red, rosy complexion, and an infectious broad smile. He came round the mill with me when I was planning the restoration. He had left more than twenty years before, and there is a ghostly quality in the recording we made that day. 'Wait a minute, there ought to be a screw here, so you can raise the stone nut,' but, of course, it had long since disappeared. He was horrified by the dereliction in the place.

EARLY IN 1979 Mr Pook returned to do some work on the machinery, and build casing round the stones. Over the years when I was milling, there was only once, in the mid-eighties, a major crisis with the wheel that we restored. It developed a wallowing movement, which made it impossible to use, as the clearance between it and the wall was only a couple of inches, and it scraped itself each time it turned. A firm of restoration engineers was working on a minor problem in the bearing on the upright shaft, and although they were experts, they could not decide why this was happening. The horizontal shaft between the wheel and the machinery was proved to be level, so it was clear that the fault was not there. I was watching the wheel closely from inside the wheel chamber to try to find an answer, when I saw that the wedges in one side of the hub were, sure enough, in position, but those in the other side of the hub had all disappeared, and had obviously been washed away. No wonder the wheel was listing so violently. It was only attached to its hub on one side. Many parts of a mill's machinery, and its wheel, are held together by opposing wooden wedges, a piece of simple technology which even I with no knowledge of engineering can understand. It must have been a wonderful invention when the principle was first thought of. However, wedges in a fast-moving working water wheel, constantly splashed by the action of its turning, do need to be watched, in case they become loosened, and float away.

Another effect of water splashing in the wheel chamber is that the block on which the wheel shaft rests can become rotten over the years. It is essential that a very solid piece of oak is used, because the whole weight of the wheel rests on it. Ours weighs about four tons. We renewed this block once while I was at the mill, and, when the wheel was jacked up so that the work could be done, we found a series of metal plates under it, which gave a certain amount of play to the movement of the wheel. There happened to be two craftsmen in the mill at the time, a mason and a carpenter. The mason advised concreting the block in place, but I took the advice of the carpenter, who said 'No. The whole system, and the building with it, move with the wheel, and, in an imprecise system like this, you need the movement and play which these metal plates allow. ' I always remembered that, and it is true that the whole building does move slightly when the wheel is turning, so that it seems almost like a great living animal.

THERE IS A CLOSE OBSERVATION of a water wheel in a poem by Sir Walter Raleigh, who was brought up in a farmhouse with a water mill close by in the nearest village to Otterton. I was often reminded of his lines when I stopped the wheel at the end of the day.

> . . . a wheel forced by the falling stream,
> Although the course be turned some other way,
> Doth for a while go round upon the beam,
> Till wanting strength to move, it stands at stay. '

A beautifully clear way of describing the effect of turning water away from a wheel.

Sometimes, however, a wheel cannot easily be stopped. Our friend the grain haulier once heard a noise in the mill in the middle of the night, went over the road to investigate, and finding a metal bucket caught in the wheel, climbed down inside to release it. The wheel started to move, and soon he was running like a hamster on a treadmill, and could not get out. His wife slept on, and it was a good hour before she heard his cries for help, and came and rescued him. He was so angry that he took the wheel off its bearings and bedded it down in the concrete base of the stream so that it could never turn again, he hoped. That was why we found it in such a bad state when we came to start the restoration.

THE PERSPEX FLOOR we put down in the gallery made a very good vantage point from which to look down on to the wheels, and to the stream as it flowed under them. The space just below the wheel is dark and cool, and is a favourite hiding place for quite large trout. I have even known a kingfisher to fish from the wheel when it has been stationary, and once, on a busy August day, I was momentarily alone on the bridge by the mill pool, and one flew up the stream towards the wheel, turned sharply, and flew over my shoulder. I exclaimed ' Kingfisher!', hoping that at least one of the many people who are always hoping to see one would be close by. But, by an extraordinary fluke, I was the only person to see it.

The bank of the pool below the wheels with its ripples and reflections was an excellent place for showing a piece of sculpture. For some time we had a terracotta figure named 'The flower girl', who sat above the pool, reflected in the oxygenated water coming out from under the wheel. She sat cross-legged, with flowers in her lap. In winter, she was sometimes dusted with snow, and for the rest of the year looked good surrounded with the flowers and shrubs of the little garden. On one occasion I moved her to the bottom of the stairs to the office for an exhibition. Returning from a stay in London, I thought how lovely everything was looking in the mill courtyard, including the flower girl. I went into the craft shop, where Martha was behind the counter. We talked about my trip, and when two men came down the stair, because of the position of the fire they had to pass close to Martha and me, and we had a good look at them. They went out, and, ten minutes or so later, I strolled back into the courtyard. No flower girl. They must have carried her out to a vehicle in full view of the bakery window where the bakers were busy at work. The police had searched their van the day before, and found nothing stolen in it. The crooks were well-known to them, regularly coming from Portsmouth to buy and steal in the west country, but never getting caught red-handed. Our local policeman saw their van parked in the next village ten minutes after our theft, but, because there had been nothing stolen in it the day before, he left them alone, and they, I am sure, made for the M5 as soon as possible. We never got our lovely flower girl back, of course.

IN 1982 A YOUNG DIRECTOR of children's television working for the BBC, Margie Barbour, was looking for a suitable venue for her first outside broadcast. Each day, the programme was to show different scenes and themes through one of the studio's 'windows'. Margie chose the mill for her OB, which excited us all, and she decided that some aspect of its activities would be shown through a window each day for a week. Glass engraving, lace-making, leather working, pot-throwing, furniture making, wood turning, and milling were all on the agenda, and Margie wrote a song to hold the story together at the beginning of each new activity. The film crew arrived on the appointed date, and set up their vans in the car park. They were there for three days and the whole place was a hive of activity. Margie warned me that the technicians were in a mood to strike about almost anything, and that I must not give them the impression that there were any dangers about the place. I had my first test when a bee stung me in the orchard as I was talking to camera, and I had to avoid showing any reaction in case the cameraman downed his equipment and left. My next test came when we were filming inside the mill, and a cameraman was standing inside the wheel chamber, with his cables festooned around him. The wheel was stationary, and, as usual, it is impossible to believe, when it is still, that it will ever move again. In the film sequence, I was to be starting the wheel up while talking to the children about what I was doing. I did say to the cameraman, I hoped tactfully, that perhaps it would be a good idea to be sure that his cables were clear of the wheel I was about to set in motion. He moved them a few inches, irritably, and while I was talking in my reassuring voice for four year olds I was watching to see if I needed to stop the wheel urgently, to avoid a very messy accident! Luckily, there was just enough room for him to work, but he showed extreme surprise at this nine foot monster suddenly churning round at his elbow when I let the water through.

I DID NOT, OF COURSE, only talk to four-year-olds about the mill. I often stood in the little passage which runs past the wheel chamber, explaining to people the stopping and starting of the wheel. This is the passage with loose boards underfoot, and I always had to bring their attention to the wheel itself, to prevent them going right past it looking at their feet, worried because the stream was flowing directly underneath them just there. Seeing children's reactions of astonishment at the sight of this large noisy monster, seeming so near to them, was extremely rewarding. They often wrote poems which their teachers sent to me after a school visit. Here are some extracts from a few.

Water wheel winding round,
And with it goes a whirling sound.

The constant rumbling splash,
Of the bubbling stream.

Mill is noisy, very noisy
In it the wheel is turning
Look at the water wheel
Listen to the sound.

Creaking, grinding, turning,

The wheel continually turns day by day, month after month. The
atmosphere's nice, all I hear is the wheel crashing through the water.

The clanging runs through my mind.
When the wheel churns round it makes a huge sound. When it turns You can
hear it churn.

Visits to the mill became a common feature in termtime, particularly
popular with primary schools. I altered what I had to say according to the ages of
the children, and to whatever project they might be doing. Topics might be
harvest, village studies, water power, rivers, bread, simple mathematics (gears,
etc.), and many others. I always enjoyed the moment when children came along
the passage, having been primed outside that they should look at the wheel,

and, even top juniors, who thought of themselves as unimpressable, would stop with mouths and eyes wide open, amazed at its size and power.

About twenty thousand people a year went round the mill, as opposed to the fifty thousand more who visited the courtyard, restaurant and shops. Many came every holiday that they spent in East Devon. Mothers and fathers expressed exhaustion at the fact that they had to take their children to see round the mill yet again, or the holiday would not be a holiday. I, of course, was delighted with this reaction, and could not hear it often enough.

WHEN MR POOK HAD FINISHED all the restoration work on the wheel I asked him to make us a fifth-sized model of it, as I was being asked to put a display about the mill and its restoration into the county show. He built a model, exact in every measurement, and it was turned by an electric pump. I used this as part of a display in quite a few shows, the most recent being when the Queen visited Devon in the year 2000. This was an event in which the marquee for the main displays, of which the mill was one, was carefully chosen and sited, and those of us who were to be introduced to her were instructed and inspected, and planning was carefully supervised. I set up the model wheel in good time, and had it turning well, long before she arrived. The marquee was emptied, except for honoured guests, as the Queen came down our aisle. A young couple with a small four-year old girl asked me if she could stand with me, so she could have a chance to see the Queen. They thrust a union jack into her hand and left. My new little friend and I were getting on well. It was clear she hadn't a clue what a queen was or what one would look like. When the Queen did reach our stand a posse of photographers came ahead of her backwards and knocked into my model wheel, disturbing the pump which was directing the water flow to turn the wheel. At the same time, the little girl kept saying 'Is that the queen?' about everybody who passed, and when I at last said 'Yes' she jumped up and down, waving her union jack, disturbing my water wheel even more, shouting 'Hullo, queen. Hullo, queen. ' The Queen, who was wearing a red outfit, stopped to speak to me, but things were a little out of control and I was very much afraid my hose was going to spurt water all over her skirt. I can't pretend I had a very meaningful conversation with her! She passed on to the next group, which included someone in a very smart green outfit. My little friend shouted excitedly 'Now there are two queens, a red queen and a green queen!'

The children come through the dark walkway,
Forcing themselves to tread the rocking floorboards.
The water rushes below them.
'It's all right', the grownups say.
They look down at their feet
Lifting them gingerly.
'Don't miss the wheel', say the grownups.
Unwillingly, they turn their heads,
And see the great monster
Crashing, spitting, rushing, churning,
Shaking on its shaft, trying to fly.
Even the cynical nine year olds
Have popping, astonished eyes,
And do not regain their cool
For several minutes.

4
The Machinery

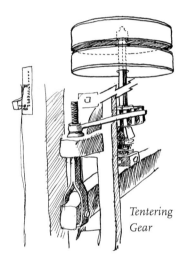

Tentering
Gear

THERE IS NOT ENOUGH POWER in the water wheel to turn the stones without gears to increase its force and capability. In very simple mills, like those I have seen in Nepal, a steeply falling stream may generate enough power directly from a wheel to grind grain (or to turn prayer wheels in the Buddhist areas near the Tibetan border.) In our mill, the slope of the stream is very gentle, although some extra power is generated by the fact that the water hits the wheel at waist level, and there is a drop of four feet which helps to turn it more forcefully. To achieve even more power there are four gear wheels on the ground floor which take a shaft up to the upstairs floor and into the stones, enabling them to turn ten times faster than the water wheel, when they are working at their most efficient.

In the summer of 1977 when we were working so hard to get the mill ready to open, the wheel was repaired as I have described, so that it and the machinery could turn again; but the drive to the stones was not, at that stage, connected. New bearings were carefully engineered, since everything in such an old system had to be specially made to size at a foundry. All the softwood casing which directs the flour down from the stones had crumbled away with woodworm damage, and Mr Pook, the millwright, made new casing for the 'wormdrive' screw, (whose name had nothing to do with woodworm, as I first thought). This lies horizontally, and is like a corkscrew. It is belt-driven, part of the subsidiary drive off the water wheel. The flour is propelled along it when it comes down from the stones, and then is directed into another shoot from where it falls into the waiting bags. The principle of this is based on Archimedes' screw for raising water, but, in this case, it is moving flour. I always enjoyed showing this tiny piece of knowledge to engineers who came round the mill, of whom there were always a fair number.

THAT FIRST SUMMER the mill was open to the public for three months, and several thousand visitors came to see it. I was on hand to tell people about it. It was intriguing to find what different kinds of people were interested: engineers, of course, and people who had worked in the manufacturing industries, and who admired the clever inventions made in the infancy of technology entirely by rule of thumb; people came who had worked in agriculture and sometimes in mills, in the days when they had carried two-hundredweight sacks on their backs up stairs as steep as ours. I used to ask them if they suffered from back problems, and was surprised to find how few of them did. I began to understand better the various ways men used to lessen the pressure on their frames when they were carrying heavy loads, such as lowering sacks from carts on to their backs, instead of straining to pick them up off the ground, and balancing them in exactly the right position, so that there was not a drag on their spines. Perhaps we do not always give credit for how human ingenuity solved such problems in the 'bad old days.'

Children who had come on a school visit often brought the entire family along to see the wheel and the milling, and to buy cakes and bread. Some visitors just picked up the brochure on their summer holidays, and had no idea what they would find. Children have always loved the sights and sounds of the mill, as their poems and comments show, and parents often enjoy explaining to them what is going on. I was specially pleased when there was a crossover between the people who wanted to see the workings, and those who came to the exhibitions. The visual impact of the mill machinery is as exciting as a complex sculpture, and has as much craftsmanship in it as in any other skilled piece of craft work.

Over the years, the mill became a favourite port of call for the people who ran a hotel in Torquay which catered for holidays for guide dog owners, and, of course, their dogs. Run by the RNIB, it provided care and outings for a number of visually disadvantaged people every year. I used to enjoy explaining what the various noises were which you could hear when the mill was working, the rushing of water in the wheel chamber, the knocking of the wooden gears, and the whoosh of flour falling into the bag. We had many exciting moments on the ladder-like stairs encouraging brave guide dogs and their owners to venture up them, and there are parts of the mill which you can run your hands over and feel exactly how they are put together. The big crown wheel in the gallery, with its individually made wooden cogs, is interesting to touch, as are the mill stones with inscriptions on them. When we had exhibitions of fine furniture, or sculpture, people with sensitive hands enjoyed feeling the designs with their fingers.

FOR MANY YEARS, a very skilful lace-maker, Dorothy Miller, set up her pillow and box by an upstairs window, and worked at making East Devon lace as she had done all her life. She brought with her some of the lace collars and handkerchiefs she had made, and even the small pieces she had done as a child at Otterton School. She said she could not work without the noise of the machinery turning, a gentle companionable sound. Every summer she enjoyed talking to people who asked her about the Honiton lace cottage industry and how the intricate work was made. She had some very old bobbins in her box, dating back to the eighteenth century. She told me how the boys used to carve them for their girls, often with messages and hearts on them, and with tiny carvings of fish and ships if they were fishermen and of sheaves of corn if they worked on a farm. They were usually made of spindle wood, she said. 'Where are the spindle trees?' I asked. 'Oh, up the river by ricketty bridge', she replied. (This is the footbridge a few hundred yards upstream.) I went to look, and sure enough found a little group of spindle trees which must be the descendants of the ones the boys used for carving their love tokens. The spindle tree itself is named from the use it was put to both for spinning flax or wool and for making bobbins. It is light and can be rubbed smooth, so that the fibres being spun do not get caught in it. Dorothy also told me how her mother used to walk six miles to the village of Newton Poppleford when she was a child, to exchange the lace sprigs she had made for tea, sugar, and essential groceries which you could not get locally in Otterton. This was known as the 'truck' system, very unpopular with the lace makers who would much have preferred to be paid in money, but who were forced to accept the system by the dealers. One of the 'days' in the BBC week of Playschool featured Dorothy teaching a little girl how to make lace, sitting in her cottage on the Green, just as she had been taught herself fifty years before. Each 'sprig', which in East Devon lace is often based on recognizable flowers, butterflies or birds, is made individually on a lace pillow, with cotton thread. The intricate design is then applied to a net backing. A sprig measuring two inches might take twenty hours to make, and would be paid for in quite small quantities of tea, sugar and dress material. Once a year, Dorothy told me, in her mother's day, a dealer would come over the hill from Sidmouth in a gig, blowing a post horn. Everyone would come out of their cottages with their lace sprigs to sell, because he paid in money instead of goods, and this was the only actual cash they earned. I was inspired by Dorothy's stories, and so I set up a permanent exhibition at the top of the mill to show some very fine East Devon lace I inherited from my mother, and some more I was given. The exhibition also concentrated on the lives of the lacemakers. The contrast between their lives and those of the people who wore their handiwork when the lace was taken to the big cities to be sold, was immense. Although the work was hard and painstaking, and the lace was often made in crowded cottages with poor light and ventilation, there was great pride in some of the fine work that was produced. The towns and villages vied with each other to tell the stories of how they had produced wedding dresses and christening robes for the Royal family, with whom there had been a connection since the eighteenth century.

THE WORK ON THE MACHINERY which we put in hand in 1979 included the building of what is known as 'mill furniture'. This consists of a softwood casing to enclose the mill stones, and a shoot and a hopper to direct the grain downwards towards the stones. Below these, the grain falls into a wide shoot named the 'shoe' which is agitated as the spindle turning the top stone knocks against it. This is called the 'damsel'. Whether or not it is true, I do not know, but the 'damsel' is said to have got its name from the fact that it chatters all the time, which indeed it does. As long as everything is working properly, it is a happy noise, hardly ever 'a damsel in distress. '

Mr Pook built a traditional set of mill furniture, and I photographed his team bringing it into the mill in mysterious sections whose use I had no idea of. When they were put together they seemed to me like a Victorian musical instrument, perhaps related to a hurdy-gurdy. The 'furniture' was made of varnished pine, and stood proudly, covering the millstones, ready to be used. Now, all that was needed was a miller who knew what she was doing.

I STARTED MILLING on a Good Friday, when the mill was packed with people. Privately, the phrase 'trial and terror' came into my head, and did not leave it for some time, but I knew I must give the impression that I knew exactly what I was about. When you are new to this particular skill, there are a few things you need to learn. One is how big a gap you should leave between the mill stones, so that the grain will make a cushion of exactly the right thickness to allow them to turn at their optimum, and grind the grain into the kind of flour you require. The stone spindle rests on a great beam of oak, slotted so that it can be moved up and down. Adjusting this is called 'tentering' By turning a screw you can raise and lower the top mill stone to alter the distance between them and get the fineness of flour you want. If you think how tiny a grain of wheat is, you will realize how small the adjustment is likely to be. It needs some quiet time on one's own with the machinery to learn how to achieve a bag of flour. A busy Bank Holiday with a great many people asking questions is not an ideal occasion for a first lesson. I certainly did not make anything that could be used that first day, but I hope at least I gave the impression that I knew what I was doing, which was far from being true.

A THICK WALL separates the wheel from the grinding area, and the temperature and atmosphere are totally different on the two sides of it. The passage and wheel chamber have the stream running through them, and are damp all the year round, so that the walls need repainting frequently; wetness trickles down them in the winter, and green mould collects. They have to be washed down regularly. On the other side, flour fills the air in a fine mist when grinding is going on, but the atmosphere is dry and a thin film of flour covers the machinery and all the flat surfaces. The horizontal shaft comes through from the wheel and turns a gear wheel about six foot in diameter called the pit wheel, for the obvious reason that it is turned in a pit. This wheel meshes with a smaller gear, centred on the upright shaft which goes up through the building. It is called the wallower, a pleasant name, though it must not be allowed to wallow and is therefore held firmly in place by wooden wedges.

One of the most frightening dramas we had over the years I was at the mill was when all the wedges holding the wallower fell out one day and the bottom of the upright shaft (which is a pine tree about eighteen inches in diameter, and twelve feet long) collapsed. Milling was going on at the time so I ran with the speed of light to the sluices and turned the water away from the wheel to stop it. Some time in the past the upright shaft must have broken and the miller of the day had mended it with iron bands and wedges, a repair which lasted maybe a hundred years. The collapse was very frightening at the time, with the force of the water adding to the drama of splintering wood and metal bending and breaking in the seconds before I could stop the wheel. One of the best things about such old and simple machinery is that you only discover gradually what methods other people have used in the past to put something right. Although I was always unwilling to call on a millwright unless it was absolutely necessary, because of incurring costs which my budget made it difficult to meet, this was an occasion when a drastic remedy was called for.

Malcolm Cooper from Calne in Wiltshire had done various repairs on the mill machinery and I asked him to look at the problem urgently. To renew the upright shaft might cost between £5, 000 and £10, 000. It would probably take two men a week to do it. The timber might cost £800, and it would have to be transported. Then all the gears would have to be stripped down and removed, the timber shaped, the shaft installed with adjustments being made to the bearings, which might need renewing. The gears would have to be replaced. Skilled work would be needed to wedge them in position with new hardwood wedges so that they were firmly in place. I explained that there was no way I could afford that alternative. Malcolm thought again and came up with an ingenious idea. He would build a false metal bottom to the shaft, shaped like a bucket, about a foot high, and insert the ragged broken ends into it, glueing it firmly in place. This seemed an excellent solution and Malcolm and a mate fitted it in a day. It has worked perfectly ever since and cost only a few hundred pounds.

A NYONE WHO MAKES FLOUR with old machinery comes to love it and feel protective towards it. I discovered one day that we have a ghost of an apprentice miller who haunts the ground floor of the mill. I was talking to a visitor who had just watched our tape–slide show about the mill's history and workings. He said he had enjoyed it, and then asked me 'But, what about the miller?' I was used to questions like that, so I replied, as usual 'I'm the miller. ' 'No, I mean a man. He milled here over a hundred years ago. He's here, you know. ' I was a little alarmed, realizing he was talking about a ghost. The man was a clairvoyant and he told me that our ghost was an apprentice who had lost an eye when he was working in the mill. His name was Ben and he lived on the ground floor. I asked if he haunted the place because he was unhappy. But, no, said the clairvoyant. He had stayed here through love, not unhappiness, because he liked the mill so much. Often after that when I passed through the milling area I would wave good morning to Ben. Not that I saw him, but I believe he is there. He was once seen by a young lad up at the top of the mill on the day when we had our puppet festival, and all the children chased the dragon away which was supposed to have drunk up the mill stream, as I have described. When we were clearing up, the fourteen-year old son of one of the puppeteers went upstairs, exploring. He came down again with his face as white as a sheet and said he had seen a young man with only one eye at the far end of the catwalk with his hands over his ears. He seemed like a ghost. It was as if Ben had not been able to bear the noise of the children banging their pots and pans and had retreated as far away as he could from the action! Fanciful, perhaps, but I half believe it myself. At that time there was another 'Ben' working in the Duckery, and when yet another came along looking for work we decided we were creating a 'home for lost Benjamins', though there was nothing ghostly about the two flesh and blood Bens, who became an important part of the mill community for several years.

Part of my run-down on the milling process during the Playschool week included some sequences on the working of the machinery. There was a head-on shot of the grain being shaken down into the stones accompanied by clacking from the 'damsel' and then the scene cut to me on the ground floor explaining how the flour comes down the shoot from the stones, and eventually arrives in a bag. I trickled it through my fingers, and explained that we finally put it into small bags, and that then it could be used for making bread and cakes. The bright lights were on the machinery, and the cameraman was rolling away, when I noticed something. We had a mouse problem at that time, and some poison had been put down. I suddenly saw a dead mouse lying right beside the upright shaft! Margie's instruction not to upset the technicians came back to me so I moved over to try to hide it from the cameras. When I saw the 'rushes' that night I was relieved to see that you could not tell what it was and I had partly hidden it, anyway. However, when the filming was all over and the team was about to leave, we had a party, and the week's work was shown on video. When we came to my part someone in the know asked 'Can you see the mouse?' Everyone paled, and stared, but luckily it was agreed that it was unrecognizable. Denys had his moment in the film, as I called out to him to collect a sack I was sending up to the top of the mill on the water-powered sack hoist. He took it off the hoist and tipped it into the hopper. Unfortunately you only see his feet!

Other lessons I had to learn so as to become a miller were to respect the interplay between the power available, the moisture in the air, the amount of grain I was letting down into the stones, and any alterations there might be on that particular day in the mood of the old machinery. If the flour was very fine it could sometimes cake inside the casing round the wormdrive screw, and then there would be a blockage. If so much flour built up that the lid of the casing lifted it could slide dangerously towards the canvas belt which turned the wormdrive screw. If it were to get caught in the belt it could do a great deal of damage. It was several times close to it. Another important lesson for inexperienced millers is that it is essential to keep an eye on the feed of grain into the stones. The 'damsel' knocks the 'shoe' and feeds the grain down into the stones at a speed that is dictated by how fast the wheel is going round. If there is a blockage of grain, or, if it has run out, there is no

cushion of grain to slow down the speed, and the wheel begins to race, putting unneccesary strain on the machinery. If the stones are close together at the time, their surfaces will be damaged, and the friction can possibly cause a fire. Many mills over the centuries have burnt down, (one reason why not too many remain standing,) and this is one of the causes. Another is that flour is combustible, and if there is too much in the air, and a spark ignites it, there can be a monumental explosion, which can blow the whole building up. This is one reason why wooden machinery is, in many ways, safer than cast iron. Wooden cogs working against each other are far less likely to cause a spark than metal working against metal. We have a mixture of wooden and castiron gear wheels at Otterton. Wooden cogs remained a safer option even when wooden machinery had largely been overtaken by metal in the late nineteenth century.

THE MAKING OF WOODEN COGS is a skilled job. I had to renew about twelve on the crown wheel when the iron gear above it slipped on to it while it was turning. Cogs flew in all directions before I could stop the wheel. (The crown wheel is the gear wheel on the first floor which provides subsidiary belt-driven power to drive the worm drive screw and the water-powered sack hoist.) This put the whole system out of action until new cogs could be made. I asked the millwright to make information boards about the process.

These particular cogs were made of applewood. Various seasoned hardwoods can be used, such as oak or hornbeam, but in the West Country, where there were once so many orchards, they were often made of applewood. Each piece of wood to be cut into a cog starts out by being rectangular, about four inches by six, and an inch and a half thick. The grain of the wood goes up and down, rather than across. This is cut into a T shape, the depth of the top of the T being, perhaps, two inches. Then the cog is shaped so that the 'stalk' of the T is tapered, both from side to side, and back to front. This is the part which goes through the rim of the gear wheel, and is held in position by a wooden peg, driven through it beyond the inner edge of the rim.

The process of setting the cog in its new home is, again, very skilled, and perhaps it is worth letting the description the millwright gave me speak for itself.

1. A template was cut in plywood to give the size and shape of a blank cog.
2. A rectangular block of applewood per cog was cut, having the grain running across the width of the cog for maximum strength. The wood was well seasoned and free of 'shakes' (splits) or knots. The outline of each cog was marked out ready for rough cutting.
3. Rough saw cuts were made into both faces each side of the blank.
4. Shoulders were sawn to reveal the shank.
5. Cog faces were rough sawn to shape.
6. Each cog was then fitted by paring away the shank a little at a time until it was driven home and pinned in place.

Once the cog is installed, its working, back and end faces must be 'trued up'. This is done by careful marking and paring by chisel:

1. A fixed marker is set adjacent to the wheel and the inner and outer end faces marked as the wheel is turned slowly by hand. These and the cog's top face are then 'trued' by paring them back to their marks.
2. The centre lines of each cog are established by 'walking' a pair of dividers round a full circumference and adjusting pitch until an exact spacing is achieved. This is checked carefully by 'walking' round the opposite direction, and when equally-pitched centres are established, centrelines are scribed on.
3. Templates for inner and outer cog end-faces are made and their outlines marked on.
4. Back faces of cogs are pared down to their marks.
5. Working faces of cogs are pared down nearly to their marks, a small allowance being left.
6. The gear wheel and its mate are put lightly into mesh and turned slowly. A marking compound is brushed on to the mating gear which in turn marks high spots on the wooden cogs. These are then dressed back. This continues until smooth meshing is achieved.

I am not expecting that anyone who is not particularly interested in simple technology will want to read this detailed account, but from all the questions I have been asked over the years, I know there will be some who will want to know about the skill involved in fitting wooden cogs.

The great advantage in being able to renew cogs individually is that it is an inexpensive alternative to buying and fitting a new gear wheel, at a cost of thousands of pounds. Ingenuity has always been the watchword of millers and millwrights, so as to lose as little milling time as possible, and to save money.

Whereas the intricacies of the machinery are not of interest to everyone, I have found that there is universal admiration for the people, mostly men, who thought up this technology. A constant comment is 'To think, they invented all this without all the help we have nowadays. No computers, nothing except their own rule of thumb and inventive spirit. 'It is good to hear people talking like that when so often the simplicity of past techniques is ridiculed.

I N THE MIDDLE AGES the records are full of the complaints of farmers who brought their grain to the manor mills to be ground, and found they had to wait, sometimes for days, because just such a repair was being done. There was nothing to do but be patient, unless, as in the story of Chaucer's miller, the time was spent making a move on the miller's wife and daughter!

There is a wonderful visual impact in seeing this lumbering majestic machinery turning harmoniously when it is in a good mood, and I have seen all sorts of people become mesmerized by looking at it. Denys did a particularly good drawing of it, showing the gnarled wood, some of it a couple of hundred years old, well worn with age.

Here are a few excerpts from children's poems. This was how the machinery affected them:

> All the cogs turning on the very old machinery
> Look like monster's teeth growling at night.
>
> Wooden teeth, moving floor,
> Standing pillars, creaking door.
>
> Cogs ticking,
> Wheels clicking,
> Flour grinding,
> Belts winding.
>
> The wheel which looks like a crown
> Has got pegs all around.
>
> Otterton Mill bangs and creaks with sounds
> Like a heavy rain fall.
>
> Hear the mill churn and groan,

Feel the flour as fluffy as foam.
Churning cogs their graisome groan,
So loud, so slow, fluming fast,
Crushing corn as they go.

(The invented words in this poem are not misprints.)

Drawing by Denys Greenhow aged 13 – 1977

Take a grain of wheat.
Send it rattling to the bins.
Release some water through your mill.
Hear the reassuring chug
Of wheel and gears
Sending it gently downwards.
Listen to the chatter of the damsel
Directing its speed into the stones.
Hear the even turning, cushioning it.
Wait for the first thud
Of flour coming down the spout.
Feel it with your thumbs, and taste
Its nutty freshness, just a little warm.
Rush it to the bakery to use
Before that grain loses its memory
Of summer sunshine and its harvesting.

5
Stones, Grain, and Flour

MILL STONES have had a long and interesting history. Originally grain was ground with hand querns, and still is in many parts of the world. This is hard work, normally done by women, and the technological revolution which led to corn-grinding being done by water power was a great saving in time and energy, occurring as it did in Western Europe in the early middle ages.

I discovered that our stones have different origins. The two pairs with rhymed dedications on them came from Northern France from a single quarry at the monastic site of Jouarre in the Paris basin. This is a famous source for mill stones, a siliceous rock known as a 'burr' which has led to these being named French burr stones. Mill stones were exported from France to this country until the quarry was played out late in the nineteenth century. These are sharp-faceted stones for grinding wheat, a hard grain, and they are constructed like a jigsaw puzzle, as the freshwater quartz can only be extracted in smallish pieces about eighteen inches by twelve which then have to be held together by mortar, and finished with a smooth topping of French chalk. They are bound by iron bands to hold them secure. Our stones are four feet in diameter.

As well as the two magnificent pairs of French stones, with their dedications speaking of the excitement of John Uglow at having acquired something so desirable to improve the performance of his mill, we have a pair of composition stones, not considered so efficient, but I was using them successfully all the time that I was milling. These composition stones were made according to the recipe of the particular manufacturer, and often his 'mix' was kept secret, and would consist of chippings held together with his own special mortar. When the stone-grinding mills were competing against the new electrically powered roller mills in the second half of the nineteenth century every small advantage that could be obtained by having more efficient stones might mean the difference to a miller between keeping going and having to sell up. The three discarded mill stones which the builders brought into the courtyard just before our initial opening have stayed there ever since, the starting point for many a school tour of the mill. ('What do you think these stones are for? Look how thick they are. It takes quite a lot of power in the mill to make them go round. Do you know what kind of power we use to turn our stones?'. . . etc, etc.)

Records from the past mention the men of Yettington having as part of their feudal dues the job of transporting mill stones from Dartmoor for Otterton Mill. They would have come down from the moor along the Teign, and then have been taken by water along the coast and up the River Otter. Land transport was difficult and so heavy cargoes were often carried by sea. Some of the early Cornish Saints' Lives mention the saints travelling round the coasts of the South West on millstones, an impossibility without a boat underneath to hold them up, but possibly they were carrying the heavy millstones in their lightweight coracles, weighed down to a point where the boats could hardly be seen above the water line.

I T IS IMPORTANT to maintain the surfaces of millstones so that they grind efficiently. This is called 'dressing' the stones. First the top one has to be lifted. A block and tackle is used fixed to an iron bar firmly bolted between two joists. The danger point is reached when the one-and-a-half ton stone is upright, and can swing from side to side unless a cushion of sacks is ready to receive it as it is lowered on to its back. Once this is done you can see the state of the surfaces. Every millstone has a pattern of grooves cut into its grinding surface to help the grain to travel from the centre to the sides, being ground up on the way. With use, the grooves become worn, and sometimes high points develop on the surfaces. There is a sturdy piece of wood called a 'staff', which is painted with food dye, and it is run over the surfaces to give an indication of the high and low points, so as to see what has to be chiselled away to get a fresh sharp surface, with well defined grooves. When I went round the mill with Norman Buckle, who milled in the late fifties before the place was closed down, he put his hand up on to a beam when we were looking at the stones, and sure enough, the 'staff' was just where he had left it twenty years before.

I dressed our millstones at the Devon County Show several times, wearing a hard hat and goggles. I did not usually get much done, as every few minutes someone passing asked:- 'Excuse me, what are you doing ?' which was the signal for me to take off my goggles and give them a run-down on the process. The chisel I always used is called a 'mill bill' (or bile by some people), and several were found in the mill when we were doing our initial clear-up. When I showed them to our local blacksmith to see if he could make some more he said that was no problem. He had made these, and had always made bills in the past. The handle we used, which held the bill steady, was made by one of the first craftsmen who had a workshop at the mill, Peter Kuh, a furniture maker. The 'bill' is heavy to use, and in the past millers did not wear goggles or gloves for the task and apparantly often had chips of stones permanently embedded in their hands. Perhaps our ghost, Ben, lost his sight in one eye through a chip flying into it when he was stone dressing.

I ALWAYS BOUGHT ORGANIC WHEAT tested for its protein levels, its moisture content, and its gluten. I looked for high gluten levels, which helps the bread to rise, although in recent years allergies to gluten, wheat, and yeast have increased and it has become necessary to offer alternatives. Sunshine is the crucial factor in making for a high protein level in a grain of wheat. The chancy nature of English summers means that many farmers do not want to risk growing milling wheat, in case the protein levels are low, and the millers will not want what they produce. (They do not qualify for the milling subsidy if their grain has to be sold for animal feed.) This is one reason why many small, and probably all the large millers buy Canadian wheat, which has benefited from long summers on the prairies. I had a strong impulse to keep everything as local and indiginous as possible, and so I always bought English wheat. Because I was buying in small quantities, ten tons at the most, it was possible to look around, and buy from single farmers. Several lessons in caution came into it. It is essential to buy grain which is certified as being free from pests. In the early days, before the organic movement really got going, I bought conventional wheat, which had been sprayed several times and had certificates to prove it. Twenty-five years ago we were most of us not so conscious of residues of pesticides on the wheat we turn into the bread, biscuits, cakes, and made-up foods we eat. However, I listened to farmers talking about the amount of sprays they were using, and also to a Tesco representative who once showed an interest in our providing organic flour to the local supermarket. He asked me if I had ever looked at a conventional grain of wheat under a microscope. I hadn't. He said I would be shocked if I did as it would be covered with residues of pesticides and fertilizers. No wonder that there are more and more people who are allergic to wheat, if this is true. It is certainly a strong case for using organic flour.

I was grinding only English organic wheat and I became very careful how I bought it. One year the local agricultural college grew some, and I bought ten tons of it. Soon there developed a loud scraping sound from between the stones when we were grinding. We had to take the casing to pieces and lift the top stone, and we found a large bolt from a tractor between the two stones. It could have damaged or even broken one of them. (Only the top one turns, and is called the 'runner stone', while the bottom one is held firmly still in its casing, and is the 'bed stone'.)

Grain was usually delivered in a ten-ton tipping lorry with a shoot for bagging it straight into sacks. It was often difficult to buy it already bagged, and even to find a haulier with a lorry as small as a ten tonner. The only way we could get grain to the top of the mill was by the water-powered sack hoist, a very labour-intensive method. Two people were needed behind the lorry to fill the sacks and control the feed into them, then one person to take each sack through the mill on the sack truck to the hoist, then one at the bottom of the hoist to send the sack up, and one at the top to receive and stack it. Lorries were paid for by the hour, and if it was raining it was a nightmare to keep the grain dry. So, a delivery usually involved five wages to get the grain up to the top of the mill, plus the haulage costs. This method came to an end when a new batch of students at the agricultural college, who had always helped with this process, told me they were not allowed to lift anything heavy. I decided we had to make a small compromise and modernise the method of taking in grain. Malcolm the millwright was about to instal a steel-lined grain bin for me at the top of the mill. At the same time, he put a pipe up through the building from the ground floor, and it came out inside the grain bin. From then onwards, grain was blown up straight from the delivery lorry into the bin in about twenty minutes. The dust generated by this method made it impossible to breathe on the top floor while the delivery was being made, so I used to stand out in the courtyard looking up at the dust vent which blew some of the dust out through a skylight. When I saw grain coming out through the vent, I knew the bin was full, and shouted out to the lorry driver to stop his blower. This primitive method surprised visitors passing through the courtyard, who could sometimes be showered with grain. We grew tiny crops of wheat in the higher gutters on the mill, as well! No system is perfect, I used to tell myself!

I normally bought organic wheat from one very careful grain merchant, John Norton, who keeps in constant touch with the farmers who are growing it, and with its quality. This is a very useful service for small millers, and John seems to have a wide network of contacts so that it has always been possible to find good organic grain not too far from home. The problem of pests is, of course, far greater when you are dealing with organic wheat, but, in twenty-five years I only had one bad experience. This was a bad infestation of grain weevils, which meant losing several tons of wheat when the bin had to be completely emptied and fumigated with a permitted substance. Although the grain had been certified, you only need a couple of weevils in several tons to multiply out of control in warm weather if the grain is not milled straight away.

I N 1989 WE TOOK PART in a race which was open to farmers food producers, and anyone else interested in natural power and healthy food. It was called The Great British Bread Race and involved everyone connected with the mill at that time. Joanna was the head chef in the Duckery restaurant. She exactly fitted the description 'feisty'. With bags of energy, and a wicked sense of humour, she had a team of helpers who all got on very well with each other and with me. Her boyfriend of the moment was a Royal Marine, which was a significant factor in our way of tackling The Great British Bread Race. The idea for the race arose from the medieval practice of baking loaves from the new season's wheat, on August 1st, Lammas Day, and distributing it as communion bread to celebrate the new harvest. Bristol Cathedral's Berkeley Chapel still has the bread oven the monks there used for baking the Lammas Loaves, and the race was devised as part of 'British Food and Farming Year'. Those of us taking part undertook to cut the wheat, thresh and winnow it, mill it and bake it, and get it to Bristol Cathedral, all in a day, using as much natural power as possible in the process, and as little fossil fuel.

Our plan of action was to cut enough wheat by hand from a field said to have the earliest crop on the Clinton Estate land. We would rush it down the hill to the mill with the help of the local pony club in saddle bags. Then we would thresh it in the courtyard, winnow it as well as we could, take it into the mill, turn up the water, and grind it as quickly as possible. Then we would bake the thirteen loaves, the 'baker's dozen' which we were hoping to make. When the bread came out of the oven, a group of Marines would be waiting with their bicycles, and would ride the loaves the seventy-two miles to Bristol, until they got to the Canal Basin. They would transfer the bread into canoes, and cover the last stretch by water, into the centre of Bristol. Joanna and I would be waiting with a hand cart, ready to run the loaves up the hill to the Cathedral, where the precentor and other staff would be waiting to receive them. We hoped to raise money by sponsorship in aid of the Devon Wildlife Trust, with whom I was working that summer on a Summer Exhibition at the mill, illustrating the natural history of the River Otter from source to mouth.

Things did not go entirely according to plan, although we did, in the end, get our loaves to the Cathedral. Five or six of us got up at dawn and went up to the field where we were going to cut our wheat, only to find that there was a heavy dew that morning, and the corn was dripping wet. We and the pony club riders went home for our breakfast, and were only able to use our sickles at about eight o'clock. I said we must leave as little straw as possible with the grain, but to cut damp wheat with hooks can be a dangerous business for which you need really sharp sickles, and you must keep your hands well out of the way. We managed that part without any accidents, and the pony club children set off down to the mill with load after load of strawy wheat. We laid it all out on a large tarpaulin in the courtyard, and began beating it with anything we could lay our hands on to extract the grain. This was extremely difficult and time-consuming. In the end we all took our shoes off, and trod the ears of corn off the straw with our feet. This still left the chaff, which is the papery skin round each wheat grain, which has to be winnowed by throwing it up in the air in a breeze, so that the chaff flies away, and the heavier grain falls on to the ground. There did not happen to be much wind that day, and our efforts at winnowing were not very successful. We ended up with several pounds of wheat and a certain amount of chaff for our efforts, which I rushed into the mill to grind. Luckily the water power was not too low, as it sometimes is in August, when water is abstracted from the bore holes near the river for the summer holiday visitors. With the best will in the world, it takes at least twenty minutes to feed wheat by hand into the centre of mill stones, grind it, and bag it as it comes down the shoots. By the time this was done it was about noon, and there were still the loaves to bake, and the Marines were already waiting with their bicycles. It is impossible to raise, knead and bake bread in less than an hour and a quarter at the least. This was achieved by Ian, who was at that time the baker, and worked very fast, but still it was after one o'clock when he brought the loaves out of the oven. The delay did give everyone a chance to have something to eat, however, including the Marines, who would be riding the seventy-odd miles to Bristol in relay, with a motorized escort. They set off in good heart, with permission to use the motorway, but unfortunately one of them was hurt when he was trying to make use of the slipstream of one of the vehicles to increase his speed. This put a dampener on the day, though luckily he was not badly injured. Joanna and I went by car to the canal basin in Bristol, and had our handcart ready to greet the three canoes as they came at speed into the basin. There was a half-mile run up the hill to the Cathedral, and we were greeted by Canon John Simpson, who took our loaves, and presented us with an engraved glass to commemorate the event. The excitement was not over for us, as HTV had been filming every stage of our endeavours, and played it that night on West Country television brilliantly speeded-up.

This story seems to me to be worth telling, as it shows how very difficult it would have been to speed up the process of harvesting, preparing, grinding, baking, and delivering a simple food like bread before the days of mechanization. And we did cheat a little. Our oven is powered by electricity, and Joanna and I went to Bristol in a car to deliver the loaves. Still, we won the prize for coming from the furthest distance with our baker's dozen of Lammas loaves.

THE FLOUR I MADE THAT DAY was not, because of the circumstances, the best that the mill and I could achieve. I have usually tried, because of the interest of most English people in having flour which is as fine as possible, to grind as finely as weather, water, wheel, time and machinery will allow. On the other hand, I have sometimes been asked for coarse flour, particularly from Irish and Scots people who like to make soda bread with it, and then it is a case of readjusting the distance between the stones very carefully. If you create too big a gap between them you cease to be making flour, and achieve something between grain and meal, known as 'middlings', which is not useful for anything but animal feed. If you have too big a gap, too, the cushion of grain between the stones acts as such a powerful brake on their performance that it takes a long time to get the grinding process working smoothly and efficiently again without too much strain being placed on the old machinery. You have to be sensitive to the dampness of the air, as well, as this can affect the ease with which the flour passes through the stones and the wormdrive screw. It is these adjustments and the empathy between the miller and the whole mill environment which makes milling an endlessly fascinating, and even a meditative experience. You cannot speed it up to fit your own impatience, to make it more efficient. You have to work with *its* speed, and the tiny changes in its performance.

I REMEMBER one of my favourite books at a certain stage in my childhood. It was called 'Jan of the Windmill', by Juliana Horatia Ewing. It had been a favourite of my mother's when she was the same age, about eight or nine, I think. Jan, the miller's son, was bullied by a bigger boy called Will'm Smith, who teased him by calling after him 'Have you got a miller's thumb, Jan Lake?' Jan suddenly put on a spurt of growth, and they had a mammoth fight, which ended with Jan on top, holding his thumb very close to Will'm's face, and saying 'What be that then, Will'm Smith?' to which the defeated Will'm replied 'It be a miller's thumb you've got, Jan Lake. '

The significance of that is that 'the miller's thumb' is a very important part of his of her anatomy. Because you can't see, but only hear, what is going on inside the mill machinery, it is very important to test the flour between your finger and thumb when it comes down the spout to see if it is as fine or as coarse as you want it, and this is something I learned almost immediately when I started milling (helped, of course, by my memories of Jan.)

My theory about how to make the best flour with the most flavour is that it is best used, like coffee or pepper, when it is freshly ground from the mill. It then has all its trace elements and enzymes intact, and it keeps a liveliness in the baking for several days, and something additional in the flavour. On the other hand, stone-ground flour from organic wheat with plenty of protein in it (at least 12%) will keep well for anything up to six months if it is stored covered in a dry place, and still be a lot better than most commercial flour ground in roller mills, treated and over-heated, which can lose most of its trace elements and flavour.

I had a phone call once from someone who said she had just moved house, and had found a bag of our flour she had never used, dating from two years before. Would it be all right?

I suggested she open the bag and look inside, taste a little, and see what she thought. I had absolutely no idea how it would be after two years! My guess was that the wheat oil might have become rancid, but, who could tell? She rang back to say it was still usable, which was surprising. One advantage of stone-grinding is that the process heats the flour only gently, keeping all the precious trace elements intact, and distributing the wheat oil evenly through the meal. Another good reason for using the flour soon after it is ground is that it can pick up moisture if it is standing for long in a damp environment. For this reason, and also so that smaller quantities are ground on several days in the week and as many people as possible can see the process I did not mind too much if only a few sacks were made on any one day. In the summer holidays this was often unavoidable, as the water power in the stream is inevitably lower when the weather is drier, and when there is more abstraction.

I once was making flour for a very exacting baker who was trying out our organic meal. He said he did not want it until it had stood for at least a fortnight. I laughed a little inwardly, as at the end of that time it was weighed before delivery, and he was buying a fair proportion of water with his flour! He gave up on it because, he said, it needed too much heat for his ovens to cook it properly, and it was not economically viable. This, too was because of the extra water content, I thought.

I N THE VERY EARLY DAYS I regarded each sack of flour produced by our simple method as gold dust. However, that is not how the buyers see it. Everyone knows how much he or she is prepared to pay for a basic foodstuff like flour. We bagged it up in 1. 5 kilo bags for everyday sale. The price of our own printed bags, the cost of the organic grain which is almost double that of conventional wheat, the time involved in grinding it into flour, insurance and maintenance on the machinery, wheel and stream make the whole process only just cost effective. Some other mills in our group of wind and water millers grind a variety of flours, build up a customer base with local bakers and health food shops, and make regular deliveries so as to make a living. In my case, I am interested in the baking side of the process as well, and so, for me, there was a great deal of satisfaction also in starting and running the bakery, using our own flour whenever possible. Making a living this way has to be a 'horses for courses' occupation. I knew I did not want to carry sacks of flour about the county, and that the enjoyment of experimenting in producing good food with what I had ground at the mill would be endlessly interesting. So with that in mind, in the mid-eighties we opened the Mill Bakery.

TEA TIME RECIPES, not surprisingly, appeal to millers, who may be working long hours in a cold mill all day. Coming in to a slice of apple or walnut and raisin cake or a wholemeal scone can make a satisfying moment to look forward to, when the milling is finished, the sacks standing ready for delivery tomorrow, the mill turned off and peace and quiet restored. There is always something to be done while you are still at the mill, and that is what makes the life interesting. What the weather is doing, which can result in too much or too little water or wind, noises in one or other of the cog wheels, meaning you need to put in another wedge to make a better mesh in the old machinery, questions in your mind as to how the quality of this load of grain compares with the last, doubts as to the economics of taking on a big new order involving delivery some distance away, little adjustments that need to be dealt with to make your sack hoist work more efficiently. All these are interesting problems which crop up all the time. Add to these the light in the morning on your mill stream or sails, and the many delights your eye is bound to rest on in a day at any time of the year, and it sounds idyllic. It isn't, of course. It can be cold, physically exhausting and financially very precarious. But one of the best things about it I know is coming home to something freshly baked for tea or supper, knowing it is made from flour ground at the mill.

Introduction to chapter on *Tea Time Recipes*.
'Traditional Cornmillers' Guild Book of Recipes'.
Desna Greenhow 1989,'90,'92,'93

6
Baking

G RINDING GRAIN seemed at first to be the ultimate reason for restoring the mill, but very soon I wanted to test the performance of the flour I was making by baking it up into bread, pastry and cakes. I always enjoyed producing meals for my family. Most of my cooking I learned from my mother and mother-in-law. My mother came from the north, and had a brilliant way with pastry which she passed on to me from her mill childhood in Kentmere. She was also a very inventive producer of main courses, graduating from the amazingly imaginative wartime cookery she managed on an old kitchen range when I was a child to the very exotic dinners she produced in later life. My mother-in-law was an inspired cook, too, and her bread and scones were second to none. She had brought up her family in Africa, and produced delicious food for them over many years. She made wonderful preserves as well, with the fruit from her garden in Cornwall, and passed this skill on to Martha, who for some years made the jams, jellies, and chutneys we sold at the mill.

Cooking for a crowd of people has always been one of my greatest pleasures. When planning the new bakery, I inevitably drew on my background, and many of the recipes we worked up, and which appear in the cookery book I wrote for the Traditional Cornmillers' Guild, were either the ones I used in my children's childhood or came from mother or mother-in-law. Many of them are still popular favourites in the mill bakery.

I N THE INITIAL PHASES several of us baked scones and cakes on a fairly *ad hoc* basis for the tea room, (named the Duckery after the medieval mill meadow), but after a few years, so many people had asked for bread and other baked goods that I realized we had an opportunity to create an interesting bakery, using traditional methods, and at the same time to supply the Duckery on a daily basis with freshly baked scones and cakes for lunches and teas.

There was a room at the back of the mill which had contained a concrete pit for housing an engine, long since disappeared. This had been belt-driven off the water wheel, together with other subsidiary machinery run off shafts whose belts were on the outside of the main building. For the first few years we used this room as a craft workshop. A jeweller followed by a glass engraver and then a basket maker worked there, but it seemed a good space for a bakery, having a door from it through to the mill, so that sacks of flour could be brought through with ease to fill the bins ready for use.

At first it seemed a matter of pride only to use our own flour for baking, but of course it was limiting, as our simple system could only make wholemeal flour. We started by baking wholemeal loaves, large and small, wholemeal scones, usually in the form of my mother-in-law's delicious, moist scone rounds, and four kinds of cakes, based on those I made at home, walnut and raisin cake, gingerbread, chocolate coconut biscuits, and honey oat cakes. They are all still made with wholemeal flour, and keep their moistness and flavour the better for it. I did much of the baking to start with, and when I had worked myself into coping with the much larger quantities needed, introduced a young apprentice, Ian, and taught him all I knew. Ian was a very swift baker, and worked in the bakery for seven or eight years. We quickly realized that you need a different technique for making wholemeal as opposed to white bread. It is a mistake to knead it too much, or it loses its liveliness and elasticity. Here is my recipe for making two wholemeal loaves.

Hundred percent Wholemeal Bread

3lb. 100% organic wholemeal flour (preferably freshly ground)

2 oz. yeast (fresh if possible)

1 dstsp. salt

1 dstsp. soft brown sugar

1¾ pts. water

Put the flour and salt into a warm place in a large mixing bowl while you crumble the fresh yeast into a smaller bowl with the sugar, and about ¾ pt. of water, warmed to blood heat. (You should be able to put your elbow into the water without it feeling hot or cold.) After about ten minutes in a warm place, your yeast mixture will be frothing and sizzling. Be careful not to put it on to the stove, or the yeast will be killed and you will not be able to raise your loaf. Now add the yeast mixture to the warmed flour, mixing with your hand.

Continue adding the rest of the warm water (1¾ pints in all) until you have a dough. It will be considerably wetter than a white bread dough, and you mix it with your hands until it has a life of its own, and will come away from the sides of the bowl. Do not knead it, but cover it with a piece of clingfilm, and put it once again in a warm place to rise for half an hour. While you are waiting, oil and flour your tins. You can use loaf tins, two 2 pounders for this amount of dough, or you can shape your loaves and cook them on a baking sheet with shallow sides to prevent them spreading too much. When the dough has risen to twice the size, divide and weigh it, and then shape it on a floured surface. You knead it at this point, but do not overdo it or a lively dough can become dead and heavy. Leave the loaves for ten minutes in the tins, and then bake in a really hot oven, about 450 degrees, for 35-40 minutes. Tip them out of their tins and cook upside down for the last ten minutes. When the loaves come out of the oven, let them cool on a wire tray, so that they do not become soggy.

I DID NOT WANT TO EMPLOY anyone who had had a training in a professional bakery school. We were using old-fashioned methods, not mechanized in any way. Kneading was done by hand and still is. When it is done mechanically more air is included in the dough and for lightness we relied on the quality of the grain, which was chosen, as I have said, for its high protein level, and the time and devotion given to handling the dough and raising it, and to baking it in ovens with no steam assistance. Too much steam makes for the soft, disappointing loaf we all know so well. In contrast, we spent a little more than some bakeries on baking at high temperatures. This way, we achieved a good crusty loaf, very popular with most people.

The mill bakers were and are part-timers, taught by me to begin with, and then the methods passed down from one to another. I suppose we have now had seventeen years' experience with baking by these methods, and the results are popular, a frequent comment being 'Your bread is the best. ' I cannot see why commercial bakeries insist on putting improvers and other additives into bread, nor why they use steam assisted ovens. My finest hour was when Phil and I were on holiday on the Greek island of Andros. We were sitting with some friends in a restaurant on the quay. At the next table were some English people, discussing bread. A woman in their party said 'There's only one place I know in England where you can get really good bread – a little place in Devon, Otterton Mill. ' I wanted to leap to my feet, and say 'Yes, it's my place, my bakery', but I didn't. They would probably have thought I was a mad woman. What happiness, though.

S OON IT BECAME OBVIOUS that we needed to increase our range, to offer different breads and cakes. Some people find wholemeal too coarse for their digestions and I was also becoming interested in using only organic flours. Our storage space and feed into the stones made it difficult to grind more than one kind of grain, and, without a flour dresser (a series of seives inside casing, used to separate flour from its bran,) we could not achieve white flour, which would have made our output far more versatile.

I am a founder-member of the Traditional Cornmillers' Guild, and this is a group of wind and water millers who carry the flag for producing flour by natural power sources. We have been going since the nineteen-eighties, and for most of us it is a very useful organization. Some of our members are young, hale and hearty, and happy to make a living grinding different types of flour and delivering them widely, without developing a bakery. Others, like me, do not want to get too deeply into flour delivery, with the problems of owning a van, and the time involved, and are anyway specially interested in the bakery side. The nearest water mill to ours which produces different kinds of flour is Cann Mills at Shaftesbury, run by Michael Stoate, a good friend over many years. His mill is extremely well-organized, and he makes regular deliveries all over the

West Country, and so I began buying unbleached white and rye organic flours from him, and continued to do so from the early nineties onwards.

I ALSO BECAME INTERESTED in spelt. This is an ancient grain, used throughout Europe from the Roman period onwards. It went out of favour when new farming methods were introduced in Western Europe, as its genetic makeup would not respond to artificial fertilizers dramatically enough to increase its yield per acre the approved amount. In other words, it maintained its century-old characteristics. It is a grain with a high protein content and good flavour, which performs well in baking, and is suitable for some people with allergies, particularly those who are allergic to gluten or wheat. Although it was little used in Europe in the earlier part of the twentieth century, it appeared again in Germany in the eighties, and became very popular, being also packed with useful trace elements. The German name for it is *dinkel* – from which we get *dinkel brod*, though here it is called spelt bread. I once met a German millionaire miller, who owned mills all over South Africa. He lived on an estate in the Cape, where he had a water mill which he did not know what to do with.

I suggested he should grind 'dinkel' to use in his commercial mills, and he was so enthusiastic he almost had me flying out to advise him on milling techniques, at a good 'to be arranged fee'. Only my commitments to my own mill prevented me going.

It is becoming easier to find spelt flour now, and some of the grain is being grown in this country. I had an idea that we could grind some at the mill. I had seen a photograph in the paper of Prince Charles eating a piece of spelt bread some days before, and wondered if he was growing spelt at the Highgrove estate. How to find out? I rang directory enquiries. 'I want Prince Charles's estate in Gloucestershire, the farm manager. You know, the Highgrove estate. ' 'No, nothing under that name.' 'Duchy of Cornwall estate ?' 'No. Tell you what, I'll give you Buckingham Palace. They'll know.' So, he gave me the number for Buckingham Palace. I explained that I wanted to find out if they were growing spelt on the Highgrove estate. 'Growing what ?' 'It's a kind of ancient grain used since Roman times.' 'I see. Well, they may well be.' She gave me the farm manager's number, and he was very helpful, but unfortunately, although they had thought of it, they were not growing any spelt. 'I wonder where the Prince got that piece of spelt bread from. But I have got some very nice milling wheat.

Would you like some of that? It won't have the Royal coat of arms on it, you know, but we like to help small people.' But the price was too high, though I am sure the quality was second to none. In the end, I found I could only get spelt flour through Doves Farm, and bought it regularly from them ever after. It has a particularly hard husk, and needs expensive machinery to remove this before you can grind it. At the Ancient Farm at Butser in Hampshire they know that spelt was used in Iron Age times, but have not managed to discover how they removed the husks. In the summer of 2004 we are going to experiment at one of their open days with different hand querns, and perhaps compare their efficiency with grinding some spelt in a water mill. It will be interesting to see if we come up with an answer.

At Otterton we soon developed a delicious loaf which is 25% spelt and 75% rye. It is a much lighter loaf than 100% rye, and has an excellent mix of flavours.

THE REPERTOIRE OF THE BAKERY increased with the ideas of the various people who were baking there. In the early days, Ian baked at great speed, and when we moved the Duckery into the stable, Mona, who had run the tea room in the early days, turned to baking on a Sunday. She was always surrounded by her cronies, and had a great sense of humour. She would never divulge her age, but went on baking until a couple of months before she died of cancer in 1998, when we found out that she was in her eighties. She was a great character. She always reminded me of the Joyce Grenfell song 'Stately as a galleon'. Mona did 'sail across the floor' rather like a ship under full sail.

There was a happy phase when for a couple of years a friend who was a cookery writer, Doreen Chetwood, and I ran bread-making workshops for children. We usually started the day by my telling a story based on one or more of the animals round the mill. The animal stories might involve eels, spiders, mice, doves, chicks and ducklings. Then the children would shape their dough animals – very simple. The amount of dough each child took from the bowl would be about the size of two grown-up fists.

Here is one of the stories:-

Mr Yeast hunched himself up in the fridge. It was early in the morning and he was very, very cold. He did so wish he could come out and get warm. Outside, in the bakery, he could hear a bee buzzing. He is lucky, he thought. He's warm, and he's going off to collect honey. That's what I need to make me grow. 'Good morning, Mr Bee,' he called out. 'Can you let me out of the fridge?' 'Sorry', called back the bee. 'I don't know how to open the door. But I'll let you have some honey when you do get out. '

Mr Yeast sighed. Now he could hear an eel splashing about in the mill stream. 'Oh, he's lucky, too, ' he thought, ' splashing about in that water. Water's what I need, as well as honey, to make me grow. ' 'Mr Eel', he called out, 'do you know how to open this door?' But the eel was not a very pleasant character. 'No, I don't,' he said, 'and if I did I wouldn't tell you', and he swam away into the dark hiding places under the mill wheel.

But the bee flew away up into the mill garden, and he collected some very sweet honey from the carnations and the buddleias and the hollyhocks, and he took it back to the bakery. 'Here we are', he said. 'I'm going to put it in this jar, and when you get out of the fridge, it will be ready for you to eat. '

At that moment Doreen came into the bakery to make some bread with the children who had come to the mill. Thank goodness. The first thing she did was to take Mr Yeast out of the fridge. Meanwhile, Mr Bee had gone off to fetch all his friends to see the bread being made. They all came flying into the bakery and poor Doreen was surrounded by buzzing bees. She flicked a tea towel about, and caught a piece of dough by mistake, which flew out of the door, and landed on the bank of the stream.

Quick as lightning, the eel came wriggling out of his dark hole to get the piece of dough. 'Help,' shouted Mr Yeast. Luckily one of the doves was sitting on the ledge of the dovecote, and heard him. She swooped down, picked up the dough in her beak, and was in at the door of the bakery with it before Doreen had time to turn round. 'Coo,' the dove said softly, 'That was a near thing.' Doreen called out to Desna, 'Can you grind some more flour, please.' 'Yes, of course', said Desna and went to let more water under the mill wheel. The eel was still hiding. 'Huh, we'll see about that,' he said, and he dived down to the bed of the stream and came up with a long rope of river weed. He managed to wind it round part of the wheel, so when the grinding stones were just starting to grind up the grain into flour, everything suddenly stopped turning. The whole building shook, and everyone in the bakery was very frightened. Luckily, a friendly spider, who was having her afternoon nap above the wheel, saw what had happened, and came quickly running down her shiny thread. With her delicate legs she unravelled the weed from round the wheel, and everything started again. 'That's better,' said the spider, 'I need a bit of rocking to send me to sleep.'

But now the eel was really angry. He swam down the stream lashing his tail, so that all the little fish hid in terror under the rocks. He made such a big wave that a poor little duckling was separated from his mother and started cheeping desperately. This time the children who were making bread put their fishing nets across the stream, and caught the duckling just before he was swept away. When the eel saw all those fishing nets he swam right off and didn't come back again. The children rescued the duckling, and took him safely back to his mother.

Doreen called out ' the bread's out of the oven' and so they decided to have a party. 'Oh, well, that's the end of my work for today', said Mr Yeast. 'More to do tomorrow'.

We held some other successful workshops for groups of mentally challenged people. There was a tremendous reward in seeing the excitement of someone who had achieved a loaf of bread they had made themselves, visible proof of what they had not realized they could do. Happy minibus-loads would depart, each person carrying their own loaf proudly in front of them.

FOR SOME TIME, Lydia held sway in the bakery, and is a brilliant baker. She perfected several recipes and struggled against bad health to produce delicious produce . After she left, Norma was the leading light. Wonderfully insistent on cleanliness, she also was inspired. Perhaps one of our greatest triumphs was when Exeter Cathedral held a two day event to celebrate the millennium. It was entitled 'Food for Thought'. The first day consisted of a series of workshops for schools on different aspects of world and local problems connected with food. Twenty workshops going on simultaneously throughout the Cathedral did manage to work up a good high noise level. I led one called 'Where does the bread come from?', and had to shout so as to get anything across. It was all good fun, with plenty of tasting of different breads and cakes, and a run-down for the children on what is involved in milling and baking. The following day was for grownups, with several very good presentations on world hunger, and on the merits of producing food locally rather than carrying it thousands of miles to its destination. A simple lunch was offered, which involved our little bakery in providing several hundred baps for invited guests to have with their 'cheese ploughman's'.

THE PRESSURE ON BAKERY STAFF is enormous, as in the spring and summer the numbers of people who come to the mill increases dramatically. There are locals, who buy the bread and cakes regularly throughout the year, and people who come down to their second homes or to stay with relatives in their holidays, and tourists who stumble on the place or read about the bakery in a guide book. Then there are the walkers and cyclists. We are on a beautiful stretch of river, as I have said, and the mill became a popular watering hole for walkers of different levels of seriousness. There are those who stroll up the river the mile from Budleigh Salterton on a Sunday, and locals from the surrounding area, and further afield. This is a very popular walk for people living in Exeter, thirteen miles or so away. Then there are the serious walking groups, meeting at the mill, and walking part of the East Devon Way, or the coastal path, or doing a round of ten miles or so. There are plenty of flapjacks available, chocolate, or fruit, or plain, and shortbreads of various kinds, too, to see them on their way.

I N THE WINTER OF 1988, my time was entirely taken up with writing the recipe book for our Cornmillers' Guild. It eventually went into four editions, and sold 8, 000 copies. I drew on our bakery recipes, and others I had collected over the years. The introduction to the section on Tea Time Baking is at the beginning of this chapter, and here is our recipe for Walnut and Raisin Cake.

Otterton Mill Walnut and Raisin Cake

8 oz. organic wholemeal flour

8 oz. vegetable margarine

1 small tsp. baking powder

6 oz. broken walnuts

10 oz. sultanas

8 oz. soft brown sugar

4 eggs

Melt the margarine and sugar together in a saucepan over a gentle heat. Mix together the dry ingredients, and gradually add the melted margarine and sugar. Mix well. Put into a greased tin and cook at about 350 degrees for 1 hour.

T HE STORY OF THE MILL over the past fifteen years has included John Early, one of a group of young people who have worked in and loved the mill over long periods, turning their hands to different aspects of what has been going on there in an informal, but dedicated way. They have done some of their growing up in the place, have got to know each other well, have had romances with each other, and in John and Emma's case, have married, and produced their son, Caleb.

John came to work at the mill at weekends in the bakery and Duckery when he was still at school in the late eighties. He went through several stages of teenage presentation of himself. I remember the time of agonizing-looking body piercing and some particularly ferocious boots. He had no idea what he wanted to do in life, and no clear ambitions, so he signed on to do a basic skills course at Bicton Agricultural College when he left school. This would equip him to become a farm labourer, but he did not seem specially interested in the agricultural life. He continued part-time at the mill. He had a relationship with someone older than him, they produced a baby girl, and suddenly John showed his enormous sense of responsibility. He left the college, declaring that now he must provide for Amy, his little girl. After that he worked for several years part-time in a routine job in Sidmouth and part time at the mill. Meanwhile I began to notice the books that John brought in to read in his lunch breaks. His choices were very wide, and he was moving through English and European literature at a great rate. Discussing books, and also history and politics with John became a great pleasure, one of the highlights of the rich and varied pattern of mill life. I was finishing a further degree at the time, and I have a feeling that John began to think 'Well, if Desna can, I can certainly do a degree.' He did a pre-access, and then an access course at Exeter University, and, by that time, he was well away. From 1999 until 2002 he was a student, but was still faithful to his work at the mill. He came out with a 2. 1 honours degree in History and Politics, and by that time he had met Emma, a law student, who also worked part time in the mill bakery. They became the Saturday team. When I was trying to find a future for the mill which would allow me to retire, I hoped that John could become first of all site manager, while he learned more about the administration, and that then he would become overall manager, allowing me to step back. Unfortunately, grants were not available to carry out the first part of the plan, and John really needed a proper salary straight away, once he was married and Caleb had arrived on the scene. He is still working happily at the mill under the new ownership and it will be interesting to see how things unfold for him and his family over the coming years. I definitely owe him a big debt of gratitude for all he put in while I was there.

AMONGST THE OTHER STUDENTS who spent some of their formative time at the mill, and contributed enormously to the atmosphere and fun in the place, there were the Findel-Hawkins boys. Three out of the family of four boys worked in the Duckery on and off over a ten-year period. Matthew was the first, a great joker with a dry sense of humour and a delightful tendency to warmth and wit. In his early twenties he was extremely good-looking, and a breaker of hearts behind and, of course, across the counter, as was his younger brother, Ben. Ben was introduced by Matthew as a good washer-up, and turned out to be a drop-dead gorgeous PE student, but, as advertised, very good at the sink. When each in turn grew away and got serious jobs, Sam, the youngest, joined us. He was doing a stage management course at Cardiff, later to be employed by the Sultan of Brunei to work in his private theatre. A memory I have, among many, is of a day when Matthew nearly got chased by our fearsome gander, Hubert. Mat and I went into the orchard to collect apples for a Duckery apple crumble. Hubert chased men more than women, regarding them, perhaps, as male rivals, and he loomed up from the river and made for us. 'Mat, you'll have to pretend to be a woman', I said. I walked between him and Hubert, while Mat, an extremely masculine male, pretended to walk on high heels, and brought his voice up an octave. It squeaked a little, because he was so frightened, as we all were, of Hubert. I was doubled up with laughter, but we got away unscathed.

When we needed yet another candidate to work in the Duckery, the boys said they had a friend who would be just the right man for the job. He was their friend, Darren, and the main recommendation for taking him on seemed to be that he was a Rugby player. I asked mildly if we really needed a Rugby player to make quiches and prepare salads. Yes, they said, Darren was a very good Rugby player, and just what we wanted. They were right. Darren was a big and very strong prop on the Rugby field, who later played for Richmond and Bristol, and might very well have got into the England team. It was true, he was a very great asset in the Duckery, and his salad preparation was second to none. He and a friend also rescued a four foot mill stone from the river, and managed to get it across a field, along the road, and into the mill car park, where it still rests, making a useful low seat for children to sit on while they eat their sandwiches. There was a phase when we had several environmentalists working in the Duckery. To make a career in the environmental field is not easy and it seems that competition is such that a second degree is nearly always needed. We had the two Lovetts, Lucy and Ben, and then Melanie. They not only worked in the restaurant and bakery, but took an active part in the environmental activities, such as helping to create our pond in the Year of the Otter, and to set up our environmental meadow.

AFTER PETER KUH, the furniture maker, had worked in the old mill stables for seven years, he and his family moved away. The little tea room in the car park seemed very small in the summer months, and I decided to turn the stables into a new restaurant. I felt we needed to keep the casual atmosphere, and that it should be rather on the lines of a bistro. We would have counter service, and offer meals all day. Initially, I let it out on a franchise, but not for long. I was very keen that we should use our bakery produce, fruit and vegetables from the walled garden at the Mill House, and that food should be freshly cooked every day on the premises. It was important to cater for vegetarians, as well. Both my children were veggies, and I very much enjoyed the challenge of cooking fairly adventurously for them at home, so I wanted to introduce some of my ideas into the Duckery repertoire. The mill enterprise had grown to a point where it was essential to have someone in charge of the cooking in the Duckery who was not me. It had become a full-time job.

The first person who filled the slot was Joanna. I have mentioned her in connection with the Great British Bread Race. She came for an interview, and it was clear she was not a professional cook, but was a capable person. I immediately liked her for her openness and humour. After we had sat and talked in the car park for about an hour, I said 'Well, would you like to come and do the job?'

'What?', she replied. 'But you can't give me the job. You don't know anything about me. ' This made me absolutely certain I was making the right choice. She stayed for two seasons, some of the most hilarious and lively times we had in the eighties. Joanna's life was endlessly complicated by her relationships, which also added enormously to the unexpected incidents in day-to-day living at the mill. After she left, Careen came into our lives, and stayed for eight years, until a shoulder problem meant that she no longer wanted to work full time. She made many good friends amongst those who worked with her, and being also a professional saxophonist, entertained at the Christmas Craft Fair every year, and at numerous other events, not least at my farewell party in December 2002.

When Careen left, after being at the mill for so long, I felt it would be very difficult to replace her. As I was wondering where to advertise for someone, it occurred to me that it might be worth enquiring at Exmouth Job Centre, before putting an advertisement in the local paper. A day or so after I phoned them, and gave the details of the sort of person we were looking for, they called me to say they had someone I might like to interview. And so, Susie came into my life. She had run her own catering business in Los Angeles, and had been extremely high-powered. When she had gone into the Job Centre a day after I contacted them, they looked at her experience – organizing the Oscar Ceremony dinners, doing parties for Jane Fonda, Stephen Spielberg and other stars, and I am sure their eyes popped out of their heads. When she asked if they had anything which might suit her, they said, 'Well, there is this little restaurant in a rather out of the way village, Otterton', to which Susie replied, 'Oh, that's where I live.' We were made for each other. She had returned to England from the States, because of her family ties, and had no wish to stay on the exacting treadmill of life in LA. We understood each other immediately. She knew what I was about at the mill, and she was/is a creative cook, used to not wasting anything, and with an endless supply of new ideas. We became very good friends, and established a way of working together in complete honesty and with a great deal of humour. We had a lot of fun, and it rubbed off on the whole atmosphere of the place for the last seven years I was there. Just about every day started with warmth and humour, and with an incredible input of energy, in spite of the fact that Susie has a health problem which gives her a really serious setback from time to time, something she overcomes by mind over matter, and the support of a doctor who regards her as a very special patient. Our different brands of humour mesh very well, hers earthy but subtle, mine perhaps drier.

OVER A NUMBER OF YEARS, Susie orchestrated a series of wonderful evenings for different events at the mill. We had an Italian wedding party, when the actor son of two of our artist friends married an Italian actress. Her entire family came over from Naples, where her parents run a theatre company, and we had a superb evening, moving into Italian song towards the end. Each summer when the Garden Opera performed in the mill meadow, Susie did a supper for those who had not brought their picnics, and for the opening of many of the exhibitions she created mouthwatering menus which became famous in the area. Here is a particularly 'Milly' one, which Susie produced to celebrate a thousand years of the mill, an evening which included story-telling, a video, and music, and a chance to have an evening viewing of a summer exhibition to illustrate the mill's history. It makes my mouth water to write it out.

At all these parties, Susie would officate with a warmth which made everyone feel at home and at ease. It was a little different from her experience of catering in LA, when she told me she once took over a multi-storey car park and created food stations on every level, using a walkie-talkie system, for the Academy Awards dinner!

OTTERTON MILL ~ 1000 YEARS
Celebration Buffet Supper

Starters in the Courtyard (weather permitting)
Cornmiller's Platter
(Roast garlic, olives, crudites, dolmas, artichoke hearts,
chickpea-coriander mousse, smoked mackerel-lemon pate,
baskets of assorted Speciality Mill Breads)

⋉⋇⋉⋇⋉⋇⋉⋇

Main Courses & Puddings in the Duckery
Waterwheel Salmon Wellington
(Poached Salmon in a delicate pastry crust)
Miller's Lattice Pie
(Capon, broccoli & mushroom pie)
Damsel Savoury Pancakes
(Soft flour tortillas wrapped around garden veggies)
Millstone Filo Roulade
(Brie, celery, apple, potato, wrapped in crisp filo pastry)
All served with:- Meadow Leat Sweet Salads
(Rocket-dandelion-clover bowl, tomatoes-sweet basil-red onion, garden beans)
& Millwheel Vegetable Display
(Roast baby potatoes, peppers, courgettes & mushrooms)

⋉⋇⋉⋇⋉⋇⋉⋇

Domesday Desserts
Summer Pudding with Posset Cream
Mill Berry Compote with whipped Syllabub
Chocolate Raspberry Decadence
Devon Cheese & Port Finale

The mosaic stands in dappled shade.
The Tree of Life.
Four birds in its branches
Reflect and shimmer.
Three look forward to eternity
The Egyptian way.
One looks back
And sees her love of life –
Martha – the garden maker,
The brave girl –
Embracing the slowing of her world
With graceful courage.
On the Tree trunk
The slug's trail of her poem.
She dances, sky clad,
As she said.
Remember, please.

7
Arts & Crafts

T HE INSPIRING ROOM on the first floor, which had excited Martha, Denys and me so much when we first went inside the mill, soon became the exhibition gallery, and housed a programme of professional exhibitions every year for the following twenty five years. I usually opened the season at Easter. The mill is too cold and damp to hold exhibitions inside it in the dark months of January, February and the first half of March. It soon became clear which kinds of work showed best in the space. Whatever was on the walls or free-standing had to be strong, to compete with the rough, low beams and the sculptural crown wheel which stands in the centre of the room, creating a powerful presence, and giving a sense of the proportions of the place. There is also the pair of mill stones, with their rhymed dedication, their surface smoothed over with French chalk. These two features were often used to enhance some work in an exhibition, and the roughness of their appearance contrasted with the fineness of, for instance, designer furniture.

The furniture makers of the West Country, some having learnt their skills at John Makepeace's Parnham House, used to say that they enjoyed the way their work fitted into the mill gallery, and we had many modern designer furniture exhibitions over the years. One year we showed a large table by John Makepeace, and another by Alan Peters. Perhaps the two best furniture makers of their generation, it was a pleasure to see their very different approaches to a similar piece of furniture together in one place.

In the early days of the restoration of the mill I had a letter from an architect in Tasmania, named Jeffrey Way. He told me that he had been evacuated as a child during the Second World War to stay with his grandparents in the Mill House. He loved his memories of that time and of the mill and, most of all, the first floor room, which had, he believed, been the most important factor in his deciding to become an architect because he had found its proportions so pleasing and harmonious.

An early idea was also to show traditional crafts which are on the decline, but this proved very difficult to achieve. In the early eighties we had an exhibition called Traditional British Crafts in Wood which was exciting and interesting. The last cooper at Whiteways Cider factory was retiring, and I persuaded him to lend his tools and half-made barrels, and to be on hand to talk to people about the craft of barrel-making which has almost disappeared in this country. The skill of shaping the staves of a barrel, binding the finished article with iron bands so that it does not leak, even though no glue is used, is almost miraculous. Other crafts in wood in this exhibition were Windsor chairs, made in the traditional way with seats shaped by an adze, a clinker-built boat, ships' figureheads, bellows, Welsh love-spoons, cricket bats, Sussex trugs, and besom brooms.

It was difficult to attract traditional craftsmen to take workshops at the mill. For a while we had a Londoner who had just retired, a very experienced basket maker and chair caner, the one skill taught him by his mother, the other by his father. He had been employed by Heal's in the Tottenham Court Road to do their basketry and caning repairs. He thought he would enjoy a quiet retirement in the country, working as a self-employed craftsman, but unfortunately, he hated the poor bus service, the uncertainty of the income, and was perhaps a little too old to respond to living in communal equilibrium with the other craftspeople on the site. He did not really like the countryside, either, and found it much too quiet. He was soon inundated with work, but could not settle, and left after a few months, going thankfully back to the city.

IWANTED TO MAKE FULL USE of the potential of the whole place for delighting people's eyes, when their response was already stimulated by the visual impact of the mill itself, and with this in mind several other spaces were soon earmarked as studio workshops. A couple of advertisements in South West Arts newsletters quickly brought responses. In the first summer of 1977 I hoped to attract at least two craftspeople to take up residence before the winter. Soon I had a phone call from someone with an Irish voice, saying that she was a leather worker. I arranged to meet her, and so Daphne Cotton came into my life. She had seen the SWA newsletter by chance, and I picked her up in Exeter and brought her back to the mill. It turned out that all she had to show me of her work was her own handbag, but it was so beautifully made that I could see she was very gifted. The space I was offering, above what would eventually become the bakery, only had access by a ladder at that time. I was astonished that, in spite of that, she said she would like to take it. I suggested she continue her journey to Scotland, where she was intending to stay for a few months, and come back with some more samples of her work. That was what she did, and stayed for eight years, becoming one of my closest friends, and a wonderful leatherworker.

That first year another long-term mill resident arrived, also through South West Arts. His name was Peter Kuh, a quiet-spoken American, and the sample of his work he brought to show me was the beautiful cradle he had just made for his newly-born son. It was simple, and rather like a piece of Shaker furniture. I at once fell in love with it, and with Peter, and invited him to join us. The space that was on offer was the old mill stable, a building with two stories. Peter used the downstairs for making, and the upstairs for storing his timber. He was later joined by Simon Raffan, an inspired wood turner, who stayed for some years before he emigrated to Tasmania. Peter and Daphne featured in the BBC Playschool week. Peter had a big part, talking to the under-fives about all the tools in his beautifully organized tool box, which he had made himself, with individual slots for each of his prized tools.

Over the years many other resident craftspeople came and went. Keith Smith the potter was there the longest, for twenty-two years, in his pottery opening on to the courtyard. Trained at Harrow, he made domestic ware with grey-blue glazes and accompanied these by one-off pieces, large bowls and lamps. During his time at the mill he was drawn into other jobs, such as dressing the mill stones and using his practical skills in many ways, putting up partitions, unjamming the mill wheel, reroofing the chicken house and coping with crises involving any of the animals. On the whole he was unflappable, and it was sad when his long connection with the mill was over.

A wide range of craftspeople had studios at one time or another, and their work included glass-blowing, print making, and weaving. Liz Lloyd used techniques based on the Catalan style of three-dimensional weaving, so that waterfalls and trees spilled out from the surfaces. Ann Bullen, another weaver and a felt maker took over the studio in the car park from Liz when she and her translator husband, Chris, returned to Spain. An unforgettable memory is of a visit from the flourishing Jane Austen Society of North America. They arrived by coach for a tour of the mill and a talk by me on East Devon lace, which had been of interest to Jane Austen when she stayed in Sidmouth. Having been told in advance by their leader, a friend of mine, that Ann made beautiful felt hats, quite a few of them piled into her studio, and she sold twelve hats in about as many minutes, some of which were worn on the plane going back to the States, presumably to the curiosity of the other passengers.

E VERY YEAR I GOT TOGETHER two leaflets, one giving background information about the history of the mill, milling, baking, the craft shop, and who was in residence in the studio workshops. The other was the programme of events and exhibitions for the season. These were our main forms of publicity, together with individual programmes for exhibitions and events. The main advantage of belonging to the West Country Tourist Board I found was the literature exchange day which takes place in early spring. Very nearly every place open to the public in the West Country, from prestigious public Art Galleries to tiny tourist 'attractions' has a table, and leaflets and posters are exchanged on a massive scale. This would be impossible for many small and medium-sized places to afford to achieve in any other way. I normally went there on my own, and crawled exhausted into bed at the end of the day having got rid of perhaps twelve thousand leaflets, to very carefully chosen destinations. The Tourist Information Centres near to us were an essential, and I also exchanged leaflets with places with similar backgrounds to ours, such as art and craft galleries, and arts centres, some historic houses and gardens, and, of course, mills. This meant that we started the season with plenty of coverage in our part of the West Country and beyond. I also circulated posters throughout the year for individual exhibitions and events to libraries, TICs, and arts centres, and sent out private view invitations to interested people on a steadily growing list.

As time went on we had an annual exhibition programme in the Duckery Restaurant, in additon to those in the gallery. It was pleasing to offer exhibition space to good amateur painters in the restaurant, usually for a month at a time, and I often left the publicity for a Duckery Exhibition to the artists. Professionals showed in these as well, and some of the best evenings we had were at the private views at this venue. Painters often had their own following, and new people were introduced to the mill and its environment by coming to one of these openings. It was easy to offer refreshments, or to let artists and their friends and relations take over the evening, quite often providing their own entertainment. It was one part of the mill's activities for which I did not feel one hundred per cent responsible and I enjoyed it all the more for that, usually acting as barmaid, and coping with sales. We took a twenty-five per cent commission on everything sold, and this, and a contribution to any printing involved, and drinks, were the only overheads for artists. Prices were not usually very high, and sales were generally good.

P ROBABLY THE MOST SUCCESSFUL sales in the gallery were from painting exhibitions where there was a following for a particular artist. We had three exhibitions of work by Ben Hartley, the quirky part-naive part-sophisticated reclusive painter whose work has been handled by my friend Bernard Samuels, for many years director of Plymouth Arts Centre. Ben's work has a following by devoted collectors, and his bright, bold and very original paintings look wonderful on the rough white walls of the gallery. Ben left the whole collection of his unshown or unsold paintings to Bernard in his will, some nine hundred pieces of work, and Bernard has taken on with great dedication and enthusiasm the recording and showing of them. I know from personal experience how possessive Ben was of his work. I once went to collect a car-load from him at his house in Plymouth, for an exhibition we were having. The posters and private view invitations were out, and the paintings were all carefully stacked by Ben himself in the car. The boot was closed when Ben suddenly said 'You can't have them'. My small son was with me, and was horrified when I replied 'Sorry, Ben. I am going to take them to show people your brilliant paintings. If there are any you don't want to sell after all, let me know. I'll bring them back safely in three weeks, I promise.' Luckily, having seen his precious babies depart, Ben was quite happy about the exhibition, though I did feel a little like a child abductor at the time.

We had several exhibitions of Beryl Cook's work over the years. She started as another protegée of Bernard's, but took off on the meteoric rise to fame where her sense of humour took her. A surprisingly private person, she loved coming quietly with John, her husband, for cream teas to the mill while she had work there, but would never come to a private view. The first exhibition we had which contained her work was in 1978, before she was well known. We called it 'Innocent Art', – innocent in the sense of technique rather than of message. Beryl was/is very conscious of trying to improve her technique, however, and she once told me how painstakingly she worked on painting fur coats, which appear in several of her paintings – 'My Fur Coat', for instance, which shows someone with her back to us opening wide her coat, to the embarrassment and titillation of an unsuspecting man, who is presumably seeing all she has to offer. This painting gave Beryl the chance to paint every hair of the luxurious fur coat in great detail.

We showed Alan Cotton's paintings many times. His children and mine played together in the water meadows and the village in primary schooldays. Over the long time I have known him he has been very supportive, including the mill in film work he has done, introducing it to his wide circle of friends, and extending his interest in it to the many local and more widely dispersed arts organizations he is involved in. Our most recent collaboration was an exhibition of children's art from Devon and South Africa which we staged in the autumn of 2002 for the United Nations Peace One Day on 21 September. This included some stunning work from school groups and individual children. It was staged in two venues, Exeter Cathedral, and the mill gallery. For our opening in the morning at the mill, we released some white doves as an emblem of peace. We had acquired them several weeks before to live in our dovecote, which we had spent time in the summer repairing. We were told to keep them in captivity for six weeks so that they became acclimatized and knew where their home

was. We had a crowd of about eighty people present. Three of us said a few words, and then Alexey, a youngster who had taken the doves under his wing and was good on a ladder, pulled back the netting from the dovecote. Not a sign of their moving out. I suggested we might clap, which could start them off. No response. Just at that moment the church clock struck twelve, and on cue, the three doves came out and started fluttering round the cote. Phew! Then everyone really did clap.

Another interesting exhibition was brought over from Florida by two friends who ran a gallery in Key Largo, where they showed naïve paintings from Haiti. They spent time going across to the island and became friendly with many of the painters. A very poor country, recently some of the work has become stereotypical and is churned out for tourists, but the collection of over ninety paintings which Rolf and Jenny brought over was very interesting, based on the Haitian countryside, and imaginative portrayals of animals, with some voodoo undertones. The exhibition did well, and also initiated a good friendship between us.

Another friendship which built up through work shown at the mill was with the Barretts, Peter and Susie, he a well-known and successful wild-life artist, and she a writer and counsellor. We had three exhibitions of Peter's work over the years, one based on the beautiful book on the wildlife of Greece which they produced together, *Travels with a Wildlife Artist*, in which we showed Peter's original illustrations. The Barretts lived in Greece for many years, in the mountains in the North-West, and some of Peter's own paintings show the wild and magnificent backdrop to their lives out there. Another exhibition of his work we showed was of paintings he produced in 1999–2000 in collaboration with the Devon Wildlife Trust, illustrating the unusual and threatened Culm grasslands. Peter was commissioned by the Trust to produce these paintings, showing the changing seasons over an entire year, and the result was a fascinating record. A proportion of the revenue raised through sales was to be used by the Trust to protect the grasslands.

From an annual programme of professional work covering twenty-five years it is impossible to pick out all the highnotes. I still have most of the posters, and as I look through them can only mention one or two which catch my eye and my memory at this moment. I am pleased to see the poster for the last joint exhibition we had of work by Brenda Carter, still life painter, and her husband, Ken Carter, sculptor. Brenda, a good friend of mine, died of cancer in 1996. She had been a great supporter of the mill, as had Ken, from the start of the project. Their elegant and thoughtful work, and their refusal to compromise to commercial pressure meant that it was always a privilege and a treat to show their latest offerings. A popular sculpture exhibition from 1989, which included one of Ken's most relaxed and memorable figures of a young man, 'The Gardener', was entitled 'Outside Art'. We used the courtyard as well as the gallery to show sculpture which was suitable for open-air environments, and included work by quite a few distinguished sculptors.

Over the years we, of course, had plenty of pottery exhibitions, the first showing work by John Maltby. He designed our logo, a very tender and intimate line drawing of the front of the mill, with a casually placed walkers' picnic, a rucksack, and sheaves, giving the relaxed feel of the place which summed it up so well. John also designed a three-dimensional cardboard cutout model of the mill for children to make up, giving a view of the activity going on in the days when the whole complex was given over to milling, and sending flour off to market.

We showed three exhibitions by the weaver Bobbie Cox. A precious memory for me is being invited to her studio to see how she was piecing together her carefully thought-up travelling exhibition, 'Woven Water', which we were later to show at the mill. A perfectionist, Bobbie uses her thoughts and feelings and her sensitive photographs to express her theme and, in the case of some of these moods and visions from Dartmoor rivers, even photocopies which show the movement of water in a particular moment.

She dyes her own wools in many cases, and works to different sizes to show subtle changes in the same scene.

S EVERAL PIECES OF ART became permanent features in the mill complex. Martha intended to create a mosaic as part of her work on the mill garden, but, in 1993 she was diagnosed as having breast cancer. She was thirty- four. Having largely created the garden in the early days, and been responsible for its growth and development, she worked on it hard in the following eighteen months, taking life in both hands and making the absolute most she could of it. She worked with plants with the utmost love and enjoyment, and made the mill garden even better than it already was. Denys and I nursed her at home when at last she became really ill, and, two months before she died in July 1995, she wrote this life-enhancing poem.

Power Animals
We were asked to find our Animals of Power
And everybody thought
That their's would be the best of all
So eagerly we sought.
Scattered to winds, North West and East
We crossed our inner worlds so wild

And the further we travelled,the more delights
Were there to meet our inner child.
Robert fancied a spider, crawling and spritely,
Janita preferred a snake for her guide,
Sam went off on his own with a lion
While I think Dancing Crow found his Scarecrow bride.
Dawn's was a Bear and Andy's an Ox
John found his Scorpion under some rocks.
It took me a while for my friend to be found
I journeyed quite widely and went to high ground.
In the eye of the sun she was basking so smug
Glistening Queen of black jet, Happy wandering slug!
I asked if she'd teach me her Medicine so sweet
I watched as she wandered o'er heather and peat
All alone she just basked in a vast universe
Heavenly blue above her and the sweet flowery earth.
She was sensual queen of her slow small terrain,
She was all feel and sensing, maybe no brain,
No worry or hurry, and no anxious clinging
Her trusting surrender just had my heart singing.
Now slug's ways are serving me well
My life in the slow lane is clearly no hell
I eat when I feel like it, search for wild food
Everything feels, tastes and smells heavenly good.
I live in a place of wilderness beauty
My heart open wide in these fields of plenty.
I dance sky clad in rain or in shine
And till Birds of Death take me, my life is all mine.

I had met and come to know Elaine Goodwin when she had an exhibition of mosaics at the mill, and I asked her to create a mosaic in the mill garden, as a memorial to Martha, who had admired her work.It is a wonderful rendering of the Tree of Life, in which one of the birds is looking back towards this world, symbolizing the fact that Martha had a zest for life. It incorporates one or two pieces of her jewellery, and the silvery line round the trunk of the tree is the slug trail from her poem. There are also Martha's dates, 1961-1995, and a line from the same poem: 'I dance sky clad'. I cannot write about this. My poem at the beginning of this chapter says a little.

IN MY EFFORT not to feel responsible for every aspect of the mill's activities, but without the finances to pay anyone to take some of it off my shoulders, I was pleased to take on an idea gaining ground in the eighties, of craftspeople running their own co-operative craft shops. We called ours the Millhands shop, and encouraged local craftspeople to join. It was difficult to find enough people whose work was of a high standard and who lived near enough to take their turn in manning the shop. We normally had about nine people in the co-op,and on the whole the system worked well. Some stayed for the whole fourteen years that we ran it. I looked after the money on a daily basis, and paid the members for what they sold. Overheads for them were a monthly fee, wages to anyone who covered their manning commitments, and a contribution to the cost of wrapping materials and card sales. The mill was saved the expence of manning the shop for six days a week, but was part of the co-op, and so took responsibility for covering a day like everybody else. Tickets to see the mill were sold in the shop. This was a small charge for people to see the workings, the current exhibition, and the permanent lace display. I often felt very uneasy about charging, but we also offered a tape–slide show about the mill, combining it with other sequences on aspects of local history. I frequently talked to groups about the mill and its workings. The amounts we asked people to pay were modest, £2 at their highest. Without any financial help for the restoration and maintenance of the property, we needed the income generated from ticket sales to pay for the whole project. Some people objected, but most wrote enthusiastically in the visitors' books, and called it good value. By no means everyone who visited the complex went round the mill, of course. Many did so once, and after that came to enjoy the atmosphere, to play poohsticks, to have a meal in the courtyard, buy bread, shop in the Millhands shop and in the studio workshops, look at whatever exhibition was on in the Duckery, and go for a walk along the river, calling back for tea.

THE SIZE OF THE PLACE meant that the potential for producing live arts events was inevitably limited. In the eighties we took part in an international arts festival called 'Concord in Devon', for which we turned the courtyard into a bowl-like open-air theatre, with staged seating for about a hundred and twenty. We had Kathak dancing, Afrikan Hi-Life music, and a number of other musical events, the most popular of which was a performance of Andean music by the Peruvian group, Rumillajta. They said they loved the atmosphere, and refused to have a PA system, preferring everything to stay 'muy naturale' with the sound of the mill stream in the background. They started their performance in the village street and came in through the courtyard, so that the sound of pan pipes increased gradually as they approached. We had a full house, and we all got up and danced spontaneously when they kindly continued to play far into the night. Our bread was the best they had had since leaving home, they said, and the only difficult aspect of their visit was that, with their entourage of families and friends, (there were twenty four of them), I had offered to put them up in the mill. They said that this would be no problem, as they all had their bedding rolls. After their performance they wanted to watch television, which was,it seemed, a treat for them. Martha and I took them all over to the house, where Phil was asleep. They watched a horror movie, unfortunately, and made themselves too scared to sleep in the empty mill. We had to turn the dining room into a dormitory, and produced risotto, and in the morning, full English breakfast. Phil was more than a little surprised to find twenty-four Peruvians in the house when he woke up!

I joined the scheme run by East Devon District Council and the Arts Centre in Exeter, named 'The Big Night In', designed to bring live arts to villages. We had story-telling and folk and classical music quite successfully in the mill and Duckery, and puppet shows near to Christmas.

In 1997 several of us organized a Lower Otter Valley River Festival, holding events in the four villages of Newton Poppleford, Colaton Raleigh, East Budleigh and Otterton, and the town of Budleigh Salterton. This was co-ordinated from the mill and kept me busy from early that year until the festival in July. We had a lottery grant, and events included a concert in Otterton church by the Dartington Trio including Schubert's 'Trout' quintet – appropriate, we thought.There was line dancing in Newton Poppleford, and a jazz evening in Colaton Raleigh, a walks programme, inter-village games in the water meadows, a day of Puppet Workshops at the mill with five Puppet Companies taking part, a barbecue on Budleigh Salterton beach, and an art exhibition in East Budleigh. I was very glad to book the Garden Opera Company to perform 'The Magic Flute' in Bicton College walled garden. This was the first year of what became a tradition. Soon they were performing each year in the mill meadow, and the audience numbers built up to over three hundred in 2002. A young company, held together by the enthusiasm and humour of their director, Peter Bridges, I was impressed when told that they usually waited until Glyndbourne was cast before knowing whether they could take part in the tour. They perform one opera in a season in gardens and open spaces throughout the country, and have built up their venues to more than forty. The 'Barber of Seville' had rave reviews in 2002, and when they came to us we enjoyed a magical and funny evening, had our picnics in the interval, and watched the light over the trees gradually fading, the wild geese flying over on their way to roost in the estuary, and the moon coming up over the meadow behind the stage, seeming as if it was to order.

Queen Matilda's tapestry
Shows Harold at St.Michel,
Raising his hand to the monastery,
Riding confident, well.
Within the year King Harold
Lay dead after forty weeks' reign.
His mother's defence of Exeter
Ended – her sons all slain.
Gytha's lands were taken by William,
Otterton richest of all.
A gift to the abbot of St. Michel
As part of England's fall.
When William sent his surveyors
To survey the lands he had won,
The richest mill in Devon
Was Gytha's, at Ottriton.

8
History of the Mill

EVERY SUMMER I enjoyed getting together an exhibition based on some aspect of local history or the environment. One which took some time to get together, and which then became part of the permanent display material, showed the history of the mill itself from before the Norman Conquest up to the present.

In the Bayeux Tapestry there is, oddly enough, a small sidelight on the history of Otterton, which would have been of interest if there had been journalists commenting on the Norman Conquest at the time. The manor of Otterton belonged in late Saxon times to the Countess Gytha, mother to King Harold. He it was who was killed by William the Conqueror at the Battle of Hastings. However, before William set his sights on England, Harold followed him in Normandy. A scene in the Tapestry shows Harold, with other of William's followers riding past the monastery of Mont St. Michel. Ironically enough, when William had defeated the Saxons, he gave the manor of Otterton to the monks of Mont St. Michel, and stripped Countess Gytha of her lands. She was widow to Earl Godwin, one of the most powerful men in Saxon England. I see the headlines. 'Little did King Harold know when he rode past the monastery in the days when he fought for William, that his mother's lands would be given away to those very monks, and that before the year was out, he would be lying dead at Hastings, defeated by the supposedly friendly Duke of Normandy.' After this, Otterton was under Abbey rule for four hundred years.

The Domesday survey, which William initiated to record the economy of the country he was taking over, has an entry for Otterton which shows that the manor mill paid more in dues than any other mill in Devon. The quiet technological revolution of the previous centuries meant that more than five thousand mills were recorded in England at the time of the Conquest, though the labour-saving change over several hundred years from milling corn with handquerns to using water power for the purpose had been very little commented on by writers.

> The Church of Mont St.Michel holds Otterton from the King. Countess Gytha held it before 1066. It paid tax for 14 hides. Land for 25 ploughs. In lordship 6 ploughs; 2 hides. 50 villagers and 20 smallholders with 40 ploughs and 12 hides. 33 salt-workers. A market there on the Lord's day. 3 mills which pay 40s.

When the Domesday entry says '3 mills' it does not imply that there would have been three separate buildings involved. Each pair of mill stones was at that time referred to as a 'mill'. What it does indicate, however, is that there was enough water power at Otterton at that time for the manor mill to be using three sets of stones. It was one of only three in Devon with that capacity. There were seventy Devon mills mentioned in the survey, ten of which were on the River Otter. The only others with three sets of stones were at Silverton and Ottery St. Mary, both surviving to within living memory.

U NDER THE ABBEY of Mont St. Michel, we know a little about the mill and its millers. They were freemen, and as such had certain privileges, although the Prior, coming as he did from a foreign country (and probably therefore resented by the locals), wrote in 1260: 'There is no greater plague in a manor than a freeman, for they wish to make permanent what is deigned as a favour.'

This Prior, Brother Geoffrey Legat wrote down the customs of the manor of Otterton, and there is a pleasing preamble to his 'Custumal' :

> Since man's memory soon fades into oblivion, it is deemed necessary to write things down as well so that events may be remembered forever. It is for this reason that Brother Geoffrey, a monk of Mont Saint Michel, at some time while he was performing the office of sub-prior, set himself, as best his infirmity would permit him, to collect together in one volume, for the information of his contemporaries and the enlightenment of future ages, everything relating to Otterton, as far as he could ascertain with certainty from the evidence of documents, and of trustworthy and faithful men.

The Custumal gives us some clues about the mill and its produce. It seems that the Prior had the right to buy from the fishermen any porpoise caught in the Otter estuary, and he agreed to pay for it with one loaf of white bread to each sailor in the boat from which the porpoise was caught, and two to the master. Clearly white loaves were highly prized, and to make them, white flour was needed, which would have been ground in the manor mill. At that time very little white wheat flour would have been ground, because of the waste involved in sifting out the bran and the 'middlings'. Most families on the manor would have eaten coarse barley bread, and have sold their wheat because they could not afford the 'luxury' of keeping it for themselves. It was different for the Prior, the lord of the manor, who was taking wheat in feudal dues, and growing it on the priory lands as well. The monks of Otterton Priory were bound by their foundation charter to distribute 16 shillings' worth of bread to the poor of the manor each week. This was almost certainly barley bread, but it is still a generous quantity.

Another entry in the Custumal speaks of the men of the nearby hamlet of Yettington paying their dues to the Mother Church at Otterton by fetching mill stones from Exeter for Otterton Mill, and cleaning out the mill stream. The stones were probably made of Dartmoor granite, and were shipped across the Exe, and then taken by sea round into the Otter estuary.

As in all medieval manors, the mill was an important feature in everyday life. Sited at the foot of the hill on which the church and the manor house stand, it faces on to the road which was even then the major connecting link with the rest of the valley. We do not know anything of the millers, except that just before Henry V annexed the manor of Otterton to take it out of the hands of the French, with whom he was fighting a war, the income to Mont St.Michel from the mill for the year 1407 was £5.16.2., about one sixth of the income of the entire manor.

THE STEREOTYPE of a medieval miller was of a man with a bad reputation. He had ample opportunity to cheat his customers. In Otterton Mill the series of grain bins on the top floor, with their Roman numerals above them, which the children and I had seen as little rooms when we first went into the mill, were each intended to hold the grain of a different farmer. However, it would have been easy for the miller to take a little out of each one for himself without the farmer being any the wiser. Millers were often accused of charging exorbitant amounts for the grinding process. Chaucer summed it up. His miller in the Canterbury Tales was:

> Well versed in stealing corn and trebling dues,
> He had a golden thumb – by God he had.

The 'golden thumb' refers to the miller's way, which I mentioned before, of feeling the fineness of the flour between finger and thumb – and in this case making sure he kept some in the process. Chaucer's miller was a scurrilous man, but had all the attributes of a miller, being very strong, used to carrying heavy sacks, turning sluice gates up and down, and loading and unloading waggons of grain and flour. He usually had an apprentice, and we find, in a lease dating from as late as 1814, that the miller of Otterton was bound to take his apprentices from among the young men of the parish. This had probably been written into the mill leases from time immemorial. He was to 'take all parish apprentices bound in respect of the said demised premises.'

He was also to grind the grain of the lord of the manor.

> He shall and will during the said term (of his lease) Grind all the Wheat and Barley used by the said Lord Rolle at the price of Six Pence per bushel and so in proportion for any less quantity.

AFTER HENRY V took the manor back from the French, it was given to the nuns of Syon Abbey, but they did not occupy it, and its history for the following hundred years is obscure. We do know that when Henry VIII ordered the dissolution of the monasteries, Otterton Manor was sold to Richard Duke, clerk of Henry's Office of Augmentations. He built 'a fair house upon an ascent over the River Otter' on the Priory site. The mill was still at the bottom of the hill, as you would expect, on the medieval mill stream. A small Tudor house built close to it may be the original Mill House. Before that it is likely that the miller and his family lived in some part of the mill itself, though there is no indication of where that might have been.

Walter Raleigh's home, Hayes Barton, had a mill close to it, whose mill stream is still to be seen, and where water power was used in a saw mill on the site within living memory.

The very graphic few lines about the movement of a water wheel, which I mentioned before, came from Raleigh, who liked the Otter valley so much that he tried to buy his childhood home from Richard Duke of Otterton so as to live there with his family. Duke would not sell, and Queen Elizabeth gave him Sherborne Castle instead, which was a better deal than a Devon farmhouse. Later, however, all his lands were taken away from him, and he was disgraced, and finally beheaded.

THE MILL, as I have mentioned, is very cleverly sited so as to be at river level, but clear of flooding. The walled garden which later became the Mill House garden, and which we had the pleasure of rescuing and planting, was part of the grounds of the manor house built in the Tudor period. Its fine Tudor gateway, with arches and uprights built in local greensand, must have been used by the millers to gain access to the sluice gates and to the head weir. In the flood of 1967, just before we moved in, one whole side of the garden wall was washed away, and with it a door with Richard Duke's initials over it, and a date of 1676. As many generations of eldest sons of the family were named Richard this does not necessarily tell us that the whole of the walled garden was built at that date. My feeling about the bricks used in the wall and the design of the main gate is that these are older, and the garden may have been created for the first Richard Duke.

THE ORIGINAL LETTERS PATENT, written when Duke took over Otterton manor, mention two fulling mills on his property. These were probably on the same mill stream as the corn mill. Fulling is the process of teasing out and felting woven woollen cloth to give it body. It is also tamped with heavy oak hammers or 'feet' in troughs containing a mixture of 'fullers earth' (a hydrous silicate of alumina) and soap, made from the plant used since Roman times as a cleaning agent, saponaria. When a survey of wild plants along the banks of the Otter was undertaken some years ago, it was fascinating to find that the soapwort was concentrated near to the sites of the old fulling mills. There were several of them along the Otter valley, working on cloth that had been woven at the substantial woollen mills at Ottery St Mary. Raising the nap on the cloth was done by running a bunch of teasels in a holder over it, hence the name of the plant. In East Budleigh church near Otterton there are some carved portraits of local worthies on the bench ends, including a Tudor fuller, his bunch of teasels and his cloth-cropping shears by his side, wearing his miller's smock. Otterton fullers seem also to have sold cloth. A bond was found recently dating from 1665 under some floorboards, when a house in the village was being altered. It gives details of the stock of Isaac Hill, a fuller. He had about 1300 yards of woollen material to sell, varying in price from 5d. per lb. to 2s.4d. per lb. This is an enormous stock. Blue dye was the most expensive, and this was reflected in the price of the blue fabrics.

ALTHOUGH OTTERTON MILL had been important at the time Domesday was written, it did not develop into a larger undertaking as many mills did in more industrial parts of the country, harnessing water power for many purposes other than grinding corn. Another factor which stopped Otterton from growing was that at the end of the fifteenth century a freak storm threw up a pebble bar at the mouth of the river; the estuary ceased to be navigable, and gradually silted up and became water meadows. For a century the local landowners tried to open it up again but the bank remains at Budleigh Salterton, and except at times of severe flooding it is impossible to see what the medieval river must have been like. Certainly no possibility of porpoises being found!

The Duke family held the manor for over two hundred years and lived in the manor house which they had built on the hill near the church. However, in 1785 the then Richard Duke, who had grandiose plans of building a new manor house outside the village, had put up the gateposts, and rode out one Sunday (when he should have been in church, said the locals) to survey the site. A swarm of bees made his horse shy, and he was flung off, and killed. He had no heirs, and the Estate was sold to Denys Rolle for £72,000. Rolle was a local landlord who was consolidating large amounts of property in the neighbourhood. Later the Rolle and Clinton family were joined by marriage, and they owned the Estate when we came to the village.

In the sale particulars of 1785, the tenant of the mill was Michael Dare, and the rent he paid was sixty-five pounds a year. Also included is this injunction: 'The tenants of the manor are by their leases bound to grind at this mill the corn and grain consumed in their families.'

From medieval times it was considered necessary to know how much grain was being ground on a manor, and therefore how much should be taken by the lord of the manor as part of his dues. The check could be made when each tenant took his corn to the manor mill to be ground.

At about this time the Mill House was built, incorporating some old shops. By the time the lease of 1814 was drawn up, when the miller was named John Edwards, the Tudor walled garden was included in the property. Milling was not allowed on Sundays, and the miller was to be fined £20 if he was caught salmon poaching in the mill stream. Salmon poaching was a cause of concern to the landlords as I have mentioned in Chapter 2.

A MILLER WHO LEFT HIS MARK on the mill and the village was named John Uglow. He milled at Otterton from 1843 to 1864, with a rent of £100 a year. He was a churchwarden and his chased silver watch and chain and card case give the impression of a man of some importance. He introduced constables into the village, a most unpopular move, and armed them with cutlasses and pistols, because poaching and smuggling were so rife. The locals took their revenge by climbing into the walled garden, and cutting down all his fruit trees. He retaliated by acquiring some fierce bull mastiffs, giving them spiked collars with 'Otterton Mills' engraved on them, and keeping them in the garden. At a lecture in Exeter museum in the nineteen seventies the lecturer held up one of the collars, having no idea what its history was. He wanted to illustrate the point that people often bring mysterious artefacts into museums, and expect staff to identify them. A voice in his audience piped up 'I know exactly what that is. It belonged to my great-grandfather when he was miller of Otterton.' And she told the story!

Uglow and his wife built up the mill into a flourishing business, and delivered flour as far away as Plymouth, sending it off on coasting vessels from Topsham. His wife Alice drove a load there fortnightly in the mill waggon, and we have a letter from her sister in Plymouth, who writes of receiving the flour safely for a number of customers, and also some cider made by the Uglows from the mill apples. Flour at that time cost forty-four shillings for a two-hundredweight sack.

It was most unusual for a village mill to deliver meal so far away, and it shows that Uglow was making particularly fine flour. By 1850 he was employing another man, and it is likely that improvements carried out in the middle of the century were negotiated by him with the Rolle Estate. These included the introduction of several cast-iron gear wheels, and the replacement of the wooden buckets on a water wheel, the one we later restored.

A rent rise prompted John Uglow to leave Otterton, but not before he had purchased the two unique sets of French burr stones on which he inscribed the rhymed dedications which later interested Rex Wailes so much:

> This stone worked the first time,tis true, May 1st, 1862
> This stone worked the first time, March 28th, 1859

AFTER THE UGLOWS DEPARTED the fortunes of the mill went into decline. A lease of 1887 with a miller named Charley Lamacroft shows that all four pairs of stones were in use, and the property consisted of three acres. The miller undertook repairs, including the upkeep of the weirs and the leat. In May that year a new pair of composition stones was installed, probably the ones I used a century later. Charley only lasted fifteen months and left, unable to pay his rent. This was the time when the new roller mills were undermining the viability of stone-grinding. Far more flour could be turned out using rollers, and the milling industry was becoming concentrated into the hands of larger producers.

In 1889 a miller named Samuel Harding took over, and the Estate supplied him with timber to repair the head weir, and bricks and slate for the building. However, three years later one of the mill wheels was said to be in bad order needing new floats and valley boards. This repair was never carried out, and this is the wheel we decided was too far gone to restore when we were making decisions about the work on the machinery.

It was becoming impossible for a small miller to make a living from the mill, and it was taken on in 1905 by Henry Long, who owned other mills, and was operating on a larger scale. Long's lease shows him planting thirteen new apple trees in the mill orchard in 1906, several of which are still standing, although a wonderful Devonshire Quarenden was knocked down in a gale in the eighties. A Newton Wonder and a Crimson Bramley have fallen, but still maintain enough roots to survive.

Long employed a miller, and negotiated over the unreality of expecting the entire mill property to be maintained by the tenant to the level they required in these times of shrinking profitability for small mills. The Estate took back parts of the complex, and some of the land. In 1924, the cattle market was moved to the meadow beside the mill, and the Estate took over responsibility for that part of the site. A hard surface was laid, and the cattle pens whose remnants we removed in our restoration, were erected. Long was instructed to dig out the mill stream, which had not been done thoroughly for some years. This is an indication that the place was in decline, as a free-running leat, as I have said, is essential to generate enough power to work the mill.

TWO YEARS LATER, a family named Rawlings moved into the Mill House, and Henry Rawlings, and later, his son Bert, were the millers for the next thirty years employed by Henry Long. The Estate continued to find uses for parts of the property, and this contributed to the business being able to continue for as long as it did. In 1937 the Otterton butcher became the leaseholder of the building beside the cattle market (later to become Keith Smith's pottery for twenty-two years, and now, the mill bakery). Frank Payne used it as his slaughterhouse, helped by its proximity to the cattle market and the railway, which brought stock from quite distant parts of East Devon. Two years after that, the Estate reclaimed the mill stable for the great horses they used in the forestry department. I recorded a conversation with Arthur Sparks,

*The Rawlings family
delivering flour in
the 1930s*

who looked after the horses there for many years. They were so big that shoeing
them was a problem. The Otterton blacksmith could not cope with the job, and
Arthur had to take them to the next village to get them shod. Drenching them
was difficult, too, involving as it does lifting a horse's head high enough to be
able to pour medicine down its throat. Arthur said he had to go up into the loft,
and pour from above! The forestry horses went into retirement after the war,
because dragging great tree trunks became very dangerous on the roads, once
they were all tarmaced. Until then, the financial arrangement for the use of the
stable was that Long provided the horses with fodder and oats, and in return
received extra food coupons from the Estate; very welcome, no doubt, during
the war.

Photographs from the thirties show flour deliveries being made with a
small pony and cart, and clearly it was mainly animal feed which was being
ground, although Bert told me when I was doing the restoration that he kept the
wheel on the right for grinding flour for human consumption, and the one on
the left for animal feed. When the Rawlings family were living in the Mill House
the garden still had its Tudor lay-out, with paths, edging, fruit trees on the walls,
and was what you would expect of an old walled garden. All that was gone by the
time we arrived in the sixties. John Derrick, the grain haulier, wanted to keep his
lorries inside the garden and bulldozed it in readiness. Luckily, the garden is
listed, and he was not allowed to do what he wanted, which would have involved

creating a large opening in the wall to allow access for the lorries. However, he had managed to make a derelict space out of what had been a timelessly beautiful garden. The up side was that we had a chance to turn it into a garden of a different kind.

I HAVE MENTIONED Jeffrey Way from Tasmania, who had been inspired to become an architect by his feelings about the room on the first floor of the mill. He was a cousin to Bert Rawlings, and stayed often in the Mill House with his grandparents as a child. When the war came, he was evacuated to be with them, and went to Otterton school. He wrote to me with his memories of his visits to the Rawlings family, and here is an excerpt of what he said:

> My earliest memories are of the Mill and Mill House at Otterton. My grandfather, George Henry Rawlings, was the incumbent at the Mill when I was born in 1933. Between 1933 and the outbreak of the Second World War, my grandfather's tenure of the Millership was punctuated at frequent intervals by our visits. . . Poor grandfather. And grandmother. They were often overwhelmed. Yet they endured with all good grace. One of the little rituals acted out on the occasion of each visit was the ceremony of the weighing and measuring of the beloved grandchildren. The weighing was accomplished with due pomp between sacks of barley meal. The measuring was carried out by grandfather who stood us against the wall beside his office desk on the first floor and carefully inscribed on the whitewash a pencil mark coincidental with the tops of our heads.

By the time the Rawlings family left the mill in 1956, the business had run down badly. Norman Buckle, who was already employed on the Estate, moved into the Mill House, and milled for the last three years before the place closed down in 1959. When we were getting ready to start grinding again, twenty years later, Norman came over one day as I wanted to ask him if the mill stones needed dressing before we started up. He showed me how to lift the top stone with a block and tackle, and the delicate manoeuvre you then had to do to ease it down onto sacks so you could look at the surfaces of both stones. He was delighted to see that the dressing he had done before he left in 1959 had left the stones crisp and ready for use.

After Norman left the Mill House, and the milling was closed down, a fifteen year lease was granted to John Derrick, to use the place as a store for his grain-handling business. He lived in the Mill House for some years, and continued to use the premises until his lease was up. We moved there in 1968, as I have described at the beginning of this book. Plenty of water had flowed through the mill between King Harold's mother's time to the present, and it had become the last working mill on the River Otter.

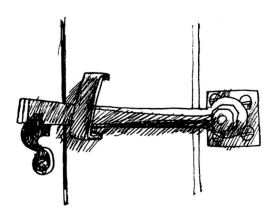

Sources

The Anglo-Saxon Chronicle, tr.G.N.Garmonsway(Everyman).
La Tapisseries de Bayeux, (Edition Ville de Bayeux).
Otterton Cartulary-Custumal. (DRO)
Dom. L.Guilloreau *Chartres d'Otterton*, (Liguge 1909).
S.F.Hockey 'Otterton Priory and Mont St. Michel its Mother',*Devon & Cornwall Notes & Queries 21* (1968)
Letters Patent 5 February 31Henry V111 (DRO)
Tristram Risdon *Survey of Devon 1605-30* (1811 ed.repr.Porcupine 1970)
Sir Walter Raleigh *The 11th and Last Book of the Ocean to Cynthia*
A Survey and Particulars of the Manor of Otterton,August 1785 (CDE)
Leases for Otterton Mill, 1814, 1887, 1907 (DRO)
Desna Greenhow *Devon Mill. The Restoration of a Corn Mill.*(Skilton 1981)
Desna Greenhow *Otterton Mill. The Last Working Mill on the River Otter.*(Dipper 1994)
Documents and photographs donated by the Uglow and Rawlings families.
Documents and photographs lent and donated by Gerald Millington and others.
Recordings made by Otterton residents for the exhibition 'A Hundred Years of Work in an East Devon Village.'(1987)

I open the flap
And they come flapping out,
The small ginger bantam first.
She makes for the grass
And the soft insects there
And an eggcup of water for thirst.
Then come the greys
And the tufty one next
Then the cockerel explodes through the door.
His matador wing plays this morning's first choice,
And he soon has her pinned to the floor.
Then out comes the Bramah, her britches adrift,
And blinks, half-asleep at the day,
While cosy inside
Bantam Two settles down
To an egg she must blissfully lay.

9
The Environment

NINETEEN-NINETY-THREE was designated the Year of the Otter, and it coincided with an idea on my part to create a pond in the lower mill meadow. There is very little still water in our valley for frogs and newts to spawn in, and whereas we have a good variety of habitats with running water of different depths and rates of flow, the frog and toad population has diminished as the local ponds have silted up (I once found a toad trying to spawn in a drainpipe in the courtyard).

Concern about the otter population led to a big effort being made to create a better chance for their survival on Devon waters. One identified need was for more quiet deep pools with plenty of over-hanging cover and deep-rooted trees on the banks to provide more possibilities for otter holts.

Our neighbours had created a small lake on their property in the hamlet of Yettington. They designed it so that the water from a small stream flowed into it, and then out at the other end, controlled by sluice gates. The same system could be used to take water from the mill stream, below the mill, and make a pond. Our friends kindly gave their time to drawing up the plans and supervising the project. The money was raised by a consortium, consisting of Devon County Council, East Devon District Council, the Environment Agency, and South West Water, with Otterton Mill providing the man (and woman) power to do the work on the landscaping.

The weather was against us that spring, and a small digger proved inadequate for the job of digging out the pool, which we planned to be over eight feet deep, with one of the banks rising steeply to give plenty of underwater cover for otters. This bank was planted with alder and willow, to give deep roots under water, should otters decide to investigate for the siting of a possible holt. The other side of the pond was designed to be shallow, to allow for a variety of marginal plants, and for different habitats for water–living insects. The idea was that, although the pond area would be undisturbed by the general public, we would encourage school visits, and pond-dipping, needing a safe, shallow side to the margin of the pool where children could paddle in their not very long wellingtons. Near to the mill stream, between the entrance and exit points, we left an island which already had mature trees growing on it, overhanging the pond itself. I was very pleased when several years later a school party found quite a few young frogs on this island.

A larger digger was hired and the pond was completed. The design included substantial stone bases for the entrance and exit points, and stone sides held firmly in wire mesh cages. A considerable force of water would find its way into the pond in flood times, but what we did not anticipate was the amount of river silt which would flow into it too. The depth has decreased over ten years to three feet at its deepest. At the start I negotiated a sale of the very fertile silt to a landscape gardener, who came and took some of it away as soon as it was excavated. We also used it in a new part of the garden which Martha was creating on the edge of the car park. Our Rugby player, Darren, carted numerous barrow-loads there from the pond. It was a wonderful tonic for the new plants, and some willows we planted from slips have grown to twelve feet in a few years, while a climbing rose, Rambling Rector, has made a mad scramble over the doorway and almost into the restaurant.

I N   SPRING   2000,   seven   years   after   the   pond   was   dug,   an
environmentalist, Steve Froom, who worked with schools and other
community groups, was keen to improve the meadow with the help of
funds from a similar consortium which was backing environmental schemes.
We hoped it could be an Otterton village project, working with the primary
school and the parents, and anyone else who wanted to take part. Steve's idea
was that we would make a series of live willow sculptures, a marsh area near the
main pond, and a bird hide, also from willow. Plenty of families took part, and
we created a hedgehog hide of arching short willow wands, and a long willow
snake beside the pond as a hide for anything needing cover on the bank. Steve
orchestrated the creation of the marsh area. It was above the water table level, so
it needed a strong liner before mud and water from the pond was put in. Marsh
plants were installed, reeds, marsh marigolds, and purple loosestrife amongst
them. A small group of us worked on a sculpture – two people holding up a ball
of willow, which we hoped would attract birds as a nesting site. The weekend
sessions when we worked on these practical creations were very happy, and
there was a chance for people in the village who did not know each other to
become friends. The greatest triumph was Steve's bird hide, made as a willow
cabin, secret and quiet, with a round opening facing downstream from which to
watch for dippers and kingfishers, and another facing trees on the bank to look
for woodland birds. I thought I might make it my summer home, to get away
from the crowds when I became overwhelmed by the pressure of people in
August!

O VER THE YEARS we had a series of environmental exhibitions in the
summer holidays. In the Year of the Otter David Chaffe, an
enthusiast who worked for their re-introduction on several rivers,
and brought up otter cubs himself, came to the mill car park with his travelling
Otter Bus, set up to show as much as possible about their lives and habits.

Recently the otter population has exploded nationally, and our river is
slowly becoming more heavily populated. A local otter-watch finds many more
spreints (the otters' scent-marking deposits) these days along the lower stretch
of the river. We look for otter footprints beneath an arching bridge on a sandy

shoreline, and picture them passing the night before on their way to a fishing foray in the deep pool nearby.

I N THE SPRING OF 2002 I met another environmentalist, Chris Holland, who lived with his family in the village. He worked at the mill for part of the summer, planting more wild flowers in the meadow, and improving the marsh area. His main achievement, however, was to create our Quiet Garden by the stream, which we decided to open in time for the United Nations Peace One Day in September. We all became involved in pulling down an old shed, under which we found a good Devon cobbled floor, and Chris planted a live willow fence beside the stream, and landscaped the three small flower beds and a space for seating. The schoolchildren came and worked on creating a mosaic path, and families had happy sessions at weekends cleaning the cobbles, and planting. We renovated our old dovecote during the summer, and acquired the doves to release on Peace One Day, as I have described. The dovecote over-looked the Quiet Garden, and after the doves were released they spent their time walking about in it, cooing. It was exactly what I had hoped for. It was a peaceful place where people could come to meditate and sit quietly to listen to the water.

T HE DOVES WERE NOT the only animals living in the mill complex, of course. We had our population of much-loved ducks, geese, and poultry. They were a constant source of amusement. I just loved the early mornings when I let the chickens out, and watched their behaviour, eating insects near the hen house, establishing which hen was the favourite for the cockerel that morning, drinking a little water, and then ruffling their feathers and walking away. As enjoyable were the evenings when I put them to bed, rounding up the difficult ones, and finally being left with just one, who you had to keep your distance from and not meet the eye of, shepherding her almost casually towards the flap in the door. Suddenly, she hopped up the step, and was in, and then you closed the flap with great speed , so that she did not turn and escape at the last minute.

We have had geese at the mill for almost thirty years. We started keeping them in the Mill House garden before I got involved with the mill, and at first

we had a pair of Pilgrims, Hubert and Emmeline, who lived in the old pigsty in the corner of the garden. Every morning I drove them through into the orchard, where they were free to eat grass, and swim either in the millstream or the river. Hubert was a very fierce gander at certain times of year, when it was the mating season, and when Emmeline was laying. We encouraged her to sit in the late spring, though she started laying – usually – on Valentine's day. February is too cold to hatch out goslings successfully, so we ate goose eggs for several weeks. Wonderful rich eggs they are, with dark orange yolks, equal in size to three hen's eggs. They are delicious in omelettes or for use in baking. The walled garden is an ideal nursery for goslings, which are tricky to rear for the first three weeks or so. They must not be allowed into the water to begin with if they have been reared away from it, because they do not have enough oil in their woolly down to keep them afloat. They become saturated, and can drown. Several times I have had to rescue them, and dry them off with a hair dryer, and even then they often catch pneumonia and die. It is particularly difficult to rescue them from the mill stream, and several times owls got into it in some way, and were washed downstream, through the bypass sluice gate. They arrived, cheeping frantically, in the mill pool. In fact, it was easier to rescue them from there than higher up, when they were still under their father's eye. Nothing would make him angrier than someone picking up his young, and a furious gander flying at you, pecking you hard in the leg, and holding on, while he beats you with his powerful wing, is no fun at all. Sometimes in the summer Hubert and Emmeline would wander across the river, and make their presence felt on the footpath on the other side. This is a favourite pitch for groups to sit and paint the river. One evening Hubert came in covered with oil paint, and exhausted. It was clear he had had a confrontation with some painters, who must have defended themselves with their paint brushes, and possibly their palettes. He looked like an American Indian for some days, and I was very glad I had not been at the scene, which must have been reminiscent of the Wild West at its most violent for the poor painters! When Emmeline had produced goslings for several years we moved the geese over the road and housed them in a shed near the car park. Somehow we got through the years without any serious incidents, though there were hazards in driving them across to the meadow each day, especially when Hubert 1, or Hubert 2 caught sight of his own reflection in a smartly painted car door, thought it was a rival gander and attacked it. The theory was that once they were in the meadow they could not get out, and looking back I think it says a lot for the patience of everyone, staff and visitors, that the place remained so popular in spite of them.

OVER THE YEARS several summer exhibitions were based on various aspects of the River Otter. An early one looked at its course from source to mouth, with input from Devon Wildlife Trust. The director, Paul Gompertz, put a commentary to a slide collection he made, following the course of the river, and we used it as part of our tape–slide show for several summers, as there was always great interest among people to know more about the plants, birdlife, and habitat of our river.

Later, when we held The Lower Otter River Festival in 1997, the summer exhibition was entitled 'Living with the River', and included a series of images by the photographer Ski Harrison, specially commissioned to illustrate the kinds of people who have a close connection with the Otter. This was intended to give a clearer idea of the connection between people and the environment of the river.

These were some of the images: a farmer in our estuary, who has to do a balancing act between making a living and respecting the unique salt marsh, of interest for its wildlife and plants; a dog walker, who walks her dog every day along the bank, who is conscious of the nesting birds, kingfishers and sand martins, and is careful not to allow her dog to disturb them; a retired water bailiff who had walked the river from 4. 30 every morning to see the sun rise, and worked for the Estate for forty-two years (He only saw an otter twice, though he saw their footprints every day, specially near the weir pool); our own Harry, who used to clear the weed from the mill stream, one of the most knowledgeable people to live near the river, and who pointed out the many attempts to control the tendency of the Otter to meander and swallow up the farming land on its western bank (In the past, said Harry, the Estate had a constant programme of using stakes to 'weir the banks', or prop them up. He commented: 'No-one does any weiring these days.'); two employees of the East Devon Heritage Service, who are seen working to improve the environment on the banks for wildlife, plant life and people, where a programme of 'spiling' – planting and interweaving willows along a particularly eroded stretch of bank – has been very successful; an elderly Devonian who lived by the river all his life, is shown removing perennial weeds from the fields nearby, and reminiscing about when there were stepping stones across the weir; a fisherman (Phil) casts his line for brown trout; and finally there I am, turning the sluice gates down ready for milling with the power from the river. This is a stunning series of photographs.

I N 2002, one of the last exhibitions in my time at the mill was co-ordinated with the newly dedicated World Heritage Site. This was the first natural World Heritage Site to be nominated in England, and the title was applied to the East Devon and Dorset coastline for its unique geology. East Devon seemed not to be playing such a prominent role as Dorset in getting the title widely recognized and understood. Richard Edmonds, the geologist in charge of the project, Nic Butler, Devon Coast and Countryside Officer, June Woodger, a free-lance photographer, and I worked to produce an exhibition showing the interesting buildings which have used the various types of rock in the East Devon stretch in their construction. I was very proud of the result of our labours, specially as it was my last summer exhibition, and I wanted it to be a really good one.

The title was 'From Rock to Dwelling – the use in buildings of the varied rocks (330 to 90 million years old) of the East Devon Coast'. There are at least eight different types of rock along the stretch of coast from the mouth of the Exe to Lyme Regis, all used in the past as building materials. We produced a large panel for each type of stone, and brilliant photographs for each section by June Woodger were complemented by Richard's descriptions of the geology. The historical and architectural background of the use in specific buildings of each kind of rock was added by me. The Triassic sandstones (about 330 million years old) near Exmouth, were infiltrated by the Budleigh Salterton pebble beds, which were laid down about 240 million years ago, when vast rivers flowed across from what became Brittany. These were used in decorative courtyards, and facings for buildings, while, moving eastwards, a layer of hard greensand was used in Exeter Cathedral, and in other local churches, in the fourteenth and fifteenth centuries. Flint and chert have been used in house building from the middle ages onwards, and Beer stone, which is excellent for carving, has been used extensively in churches, and for most of the sculptures in Exeter Cathedral. Some of the houses in Lyme Bay are built of the blue lias limestone found near Lyme Regis.

After the exhibition was on view through the summer holidays at the mill, it had a showing on the cliffs near Exmouth, and was seen by Prince Charles when he came to unveil a plinth, marking one end of the stretch of coast of the World Heritage Site. With his enthusiasm for architecture, he seemed extremely interested.

IN 2002 WE BECAME INVOLVED in the movement for local food production and sales, and selling organic produce. We turned what had been the pottery into an organic food shop, selling our baked goods from there rather than from the bakery, and we stocked up with organic vegetables and meats. These began to sell well, and we soon decided to have a regular stall selling our own baked cakes and bread at Exmouth farmers' market. Many people who liked our produce found it much more convenient to buy it in the centre of town, and it also introduced more people to our baked goods who knew nothing about them before. This did surprise me, as we had been selling them for seventeen years from the mill and from other outlets, and Exmouth is only six miles from Otterton. It just shows that the idea of selling local produce has to be pushed if it is to make a real impact on the way we shop.

The children do not need
The swirling river with its bridge
For poohsticks.
A few planks
Hardly four feet wide
Will do.
Hundreds of them play it there
Running from side to side,
Though it only means
Three steps,
Quite possible to do,
If you're no more than two.
But even fun when
You're as much as ten.

10
Winding Down

I HAD BEEN WORRIED for some time as to how it would be possible to stop running the mill. A chief executive with a wage of £100 a week might not be an easy person to find. At the same time I had been at it for twenty-five years and my joints were rebelling at the heavy turning of sluice wheels and lifting of sacks. Also, the necessary paperwork to be done on a daily basis was increasing all the time.

The mill had become a place much-loved by thousands of people, who came there again and again. We were into the third generation of pooh-stick players. People in their twenties told me how they had first come on a school trip and had then brought their parents, and were now bringing their children.

Though this sounds a success, and certainly was in the brief I had set for the place, financially it had never been a profit-making enterprise, which made it even more difficult to pass on. The overheads of running a site as large as this one, with its limitations on parking space, the upkeep of the meadows, mill and millstream, the limited access to the upper floors, the different parts of the enterprise which involved a large wage bill, and the lack of initial investment available, all added up to a very careful eye having to be kept on the annual finances. I was a fanatic, and completely besotted by the place, which had my name written on it for good or ill, and this was another reason it might be difficult to get someone else to take it over in the same or a similar spirit. It might also be difficult to turn it into a highly commercial place, even if a new lease allowed that. Similar centres in Devon with an arts and crafts briefing were subsidised, and if the place went the way of being only a water-powered mill and bakery, I knew from other members of our Guild how precarious trying to make a living that way could be. We were able to keep our heads above water by dint of the peculiar mix we were offering, I reckoned, and by the feeling of freedom there was in the place. Many of the people who worked there over the years put their energies fully into it because they liked the atmosphere and, they said, the laid back approach, and this carried over into their dealings with visitors. We had between us all built up a good impetus to carry the place forward. It was a place to which people came 'expecting the answer "yes"'.

I N THE AUTUMN OF 2001 two of the directors, Peter and Joan Speke, who had supported and helped me through many years, and a friend who had a great deal of experience in handling the transfer of businesses, John George, talked through the idea of turning the place into a CharitableTrust.

After plenty of discussion we decided it would be a good idea to take on more environmental activities, and perhaps to team up with an environmental Charity based in East Devon. I had no intention of our dropping our arts activities, and it looked as though I might stay on to organize those, and continue milling for a shortish time. I was, as I say, beginning to find the work of turning sluice wheels and lifting sacks a little heavy for my seventy-year-old frame. I knew that a living could be built up by someone young and strong who would mill, supervise the bakery, and go out to find new markets for flour. The fact that there was already an outlet on the site for the flour and baked goods, and that the local farmers' markets were flourishing, and asking for our bread and cakes, made this realistic.

WITH ALL THESE PLANS, there was a danger of making the organization of the place very fragmented, and I could see that it would still be difficult for me to back away from it. I might find myself only dealing with what I really hated, the administration, with all the dreaded form-filling it involved. There was another reason for not wanting to stay in that particular part of Devon for long. My marriage had collapsed, and I was no longer living in the Mill House. I had plenty of support from good friends, and was lucky enough to stay with one of them who had recently lost her husband, not far away in Branscombe. Life took on a surreal aspect, all the same, and I soon realized I did not want to stay in East Devon for the two years it would take to get the mill set into its new pattern, particularly on the other side of the road from the Mill House.

IN THE SPRING OF 2002 we discovered an environmental Charity named Education Earthwise. They helped organizations such as ours to establish rangers on their sites to run courses on various environmental topics. We were well-placed to take part in this kind of venture, with the river, mill stream, pond and meadows. The mill is about a mile from the estuary, and close to the agricultural college which runs environmental courses, and with whom I have always had close connections.

I have mentioned an environmentalist named Chris Holland. He co-ordinated the Quiet Garden, and the improvement of the marsh area, and later in the summer he and Ann Bullen, the weaver and felt-maker, and a number of visitors and 'mill people' made a yurt from felt, with each panel having an individual person's design. In spite of my anxiety about the finances and the future, I was glad that what I knew would be my last full-time year at the mill was fulfilling for quite a few people as well as myself.

Meanwhile I was very sad to be leaving a place where I felt we had highlighted simple pleasures, with no hype involved – the very opposite to the idea of an 'attraction' – depending for people's enjoyment on small visual delights, and the appreciation of the old working mill itself, grinding in its time-honoured way.

Another part of the plan to 'go the environmental route' was that we started our organic and local produce food shop. Keith Smith the potter, who had been at the mill for over twenty years, had taken on a full-time job in Exeter as a picture framer, and had left. The new shop opened in time for the 2002 season.

I feel very strongly that it makes sense for food not to be transported thousands or even hundreds of miles. Using local produce saves congestion on the roads, and helps conserve non-renewable energy sources. It also encourages local producers, and the mill itself comes into that category, churning out organic flour for sale in a small area. Admittedly there is the counter-argument that third world countries need western markets in which to sell their produce, to avoid their small producers being swamped by the multi-nationals. We, however, decided to stick to food produced in the West Country, the nearer home the better. Through the summer it gradually became known that we were selling organic produce. Now the bakery is combined with it and is doing even better than before.

ONE DAY IN JUNE I saw some people I knew sitting in the courtyard, having coffee. They were Bob Butler and Clare Stein. I knew them both, Bob and I having served together for some years on the committee of Devon Arts Forum, and Clare being an Arts Officer with whom I had had dealings over funding. I had met them recently on several arts-oriented occasions, and had heard that they were now partners. I joined them for coffee, and they tentatively asked if I was still thinking of stepping back from the mill. They told me how they loved the atmosphere of the place, and said that Clare had a dream of running her own gallery. There was a wide circle of artists and craftsmen with whom they were in contact. With their arts credentials I knew this to be true.

With their interest I felt a sense of enormous relief that we might not have to go on struggling to find a future for my beloved mill. I really did not want to find it a burden, when it had been for so long such a joy. I had every reason to leave that part of Devon on a high note, at least as far as my relationship with the mill project was concerned. There was a great deal to be considered, though.

I STILL FELT VERY STRONGLY about the initial ideal which had led me to restore the place. I had wanted it to show itself in its true light for people to discover for themselves. The production of flour by the traditional method of harnessing natural power was an important part of it. The lovely surroundings were, if left to themselves, soul-enhancing, and the gradual changes over a quarter of a century had not been too jarring. People found a value in this gentleness which they did not always expect, and I felt that was important, and was pleased to hear them say they felt it, too. But, as I told myself, very few people have a chance to realise their dream over such a long time, and whatever the future, I would have to accept that other dreams could work, too.

I had been incredibly lucky to have had this time, a watcher as well as a participant, in something I really thought important. People well qualified to take over part of the mill's activities were interested, with the advantage of being twenty and thirty years respectively younger than me, and this was appealing, though I was hoping very much that they would continue a most important aspect of the place, the milling and the baking.

Of course I also felt responsible for the future of the people working at the mill. Many of them were my closest friends, and we had long associations. While negotiations continued, two other partners joined Bob and Clare, Lisa and Simon, very sensitive to the environmental aspects of the place. When I saw Simon bird-watching in the car park, and identifying more varieties than I had ever seen, I was happy about that aspect of the changeover.

It was important that the milling should be handed on to someone who had an empathy with the old machinery, and who would regard the stream, wheel and gears as their own, and would take full responsibility for them, and nurture them as I had – someone who realized that there was a patient skill needed not to strain the ancient 'animal', and to help it to do its work as well as it could, while loving it in the process and understanding its quirks and secrets. I wanted all the previous millers, including our ghost, Ben, to rest easy.

N EGOTIATIONS CONTINUED through the autumn, and until the end of the year, while my own life was simultaneously undergoing the long process of difficult change. I had wonderful support from friends and family, however, and frequent oases of staying in lovely places away from the business of winding up my part in the previous quarter of a century at the mill. Even so, it was a very worrying and anxious time, with varying effects on different members of the mill community. Nanna the potter and Ann the weaver stayed on. Norma and Brenda in the bakery left when I did, deciding it was the end of a chapter for them. Susie in the Duckery felt the same. She and I had worked very closely and our ways were interwoven. Having worried about John Early, who had been at the mill for so long, it was good that he made such a seamless and happy changeover.

Bob and Clare, Simon and Lisa have created an upmarket, selling craft gallery, using part of the interior of the mill building, and introducing new artists and craftspeople. The restaurant and bakery continue, and when I visit, I meet many old friends, both visitors and staff, and feel that the place has kept its integrity, and has moved on happily.

I remember one year, when we were already extremely busy, that I marvelled at a wren, who made her nest above the doorway into the old bakery. She was very discreet at feeding her young during the day, when numerous people went in and out through the door, but as soon as the mill was closed, and I might be sitting on the seat near the bakery enjoying the silence, she boldly swooped and chirruped, and flew in and out, seeming to say that the place was still itself, after all the people had gone. I used to feel that a thrush who sang in the early mornings several springs running, in the tree directly above Martha's mosaic, was giving out the same message.

D ECEMBER 29TH 2002 was the evening of my farewell party, which we held in the Gallery. There was not much planning for it. It was a get-together of about a hundred people who had been involved in one way and another with the place over a long time. There were some artists and craftsmen who had enjoyed showing their work, they said, in this odd, quirky space. People were there who had worked at the mill in the past . Carreen who had cooked in the Duckery, played her saxophone with Terry, her partner. Susie, of course, was very much in evidence, and produced some mouth-watering

food. Sarah, who worked in the Duckery, and was studying voice at Birmingham, sang a sad lament by Purcell (she told me she chose it because it was the only piece she could sing unaccompanied!). My friend Susie Barrett, a poet and writer, whose husband Peter had shown his paintings several times in the gallery, wrote a poem for the occasion, which moved me very much, and my son Denys overwhelmed me with the nice things he said in his speech. Jed, who has illustrated this book, made brilliant sketches of us all. We showed the old videos of the restoration of the mill, and of the Playschool week. (Someone who saw me on the video asked who this presenter woman was! The changes that twenty years can bring!) Watching that sequence, too, were our two original resident craftspeople, Peter and Daphne. It really was a magical drawing together of a long, long stretch of time, not maudlin or too nostalgic, just fun, as so much had been over those twenty- five years.

WHO ARE WE?

A poem for Desna on leaving the mill, December, 2002,
with love from Susie Barrett

A single autumn leaf
eddies and twirls
in the mill leat.
One life ended.

Combed weeds
Stream like tresses
Or Ophelia's billowing dress.
A daughter
Drowned in sadness.
A mosaic of memories
Below the dove cot.

Once upon a time
The wheel stopped turning.
No creaking, grinding,
save the scattering of corn
by rats.
Wedges of weeds
clogged the stream
to silence. Dereliction.
Until her hand glanced

Upon the possibility
Of new life.
Turned the wheel again.
Water flowed in,
and the breath of life,
to feed and flower
the spirit.

The dove, holding peace,
learns where
and how to fly
from home,
Pinprick steps
And pecks
The wire pulled aside
To let it free.

The wheel turns again.
Another life begins.
Who are we to dare
To love and lose?
We only know that
Love goes on.

Appendix
Nuts and Bolts

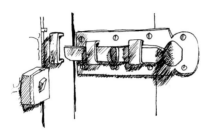

IT IS PROBABLY WORTH HANDING ON some of the problems I had in making the mill project work on a day-to day basis. Lack of funds, more and more people visiting, the increase in bureaucracy over the years, and my own age, made the administration more and more complicated. Towards the end I was not enjoying this part of the operation, and the amount of time it took to conform with the demands of the 'powers that be' in ways which were really designed for far bigger operators, or for totally commercial operations, became quite trying. Small maverick enterprises working to an ideal, without subsidy, are not recognised, on the whole, as needing consideration by bureaucracy, although, I am glad to say that all the organizations I worked *with* were, from beginning to end, extremely supportive. To name some of them, East Devon District Council, the Coast and Countryside Service, Devon County Council, Devon Wildlife Trust, South West Arts and the Environment Agency all understood what we were trying to do at the mill. As so many locals visited, most of the people in the organizations I worked with knew the place well.

For the purposes of the Inland Revenue and Customs and Excise the mill enterprise was a small business. It was never profit-making, for reasons that I have tried to explain, but several times when it seemed a good idea to turn it into a Charity the deciding factor was how much extra work that would involve for the administrator (me). Also, a visit from the Charity Commissioners convinced me that some of what they wanted me to do was actually quite uncharitable. They insisted that the Charity should get some income guaranteed from all the exhibitions we held. As my system was to take a commission from exhibitors on sales, and a contribution to costs, most of the income only came to us when work was sold. The commissioners wanted me to hire out the gallery, and take a rent, leaving the hirers to organize the whole thing themselves. This would have taken the control of quality entirely out of my hands, and would have made it impossible to get grants from any other source, since it would have created a completely commercial gallery. I was frankly horrified, especially when I was asked if artists showing in the restaurant 'got anything' out of selling work there – money, it was implied, which should go to the Charity. My aim was to help artists, a far more charitable intention than the commissioners were proposing. When I spoke privately to the more senior member of the inspection team at the end of the visit, he told me he realised *I* was the charity running the place, and advised me to carry on as I was. He said, 'It will only take up extra time and money becoming a Charity, which you probably won't recoup from the saving you will make on the business rates. '

As the years went by there was more and more form-filling to deal with, and more and more categories of conformity to meet, particularly once EU legislation increased. There was also the changing legislation on operating P.A.Y.E. The numbers of employees at the mill varied according to the seasons, but end of year returns usually listed as many as twenty-five people, some of whom had worked throughout the year, most part-time, some had come and gone in the busy summer months, some were students working in their holidays, others were on family tax credits, a few from time to time on long-term sick leave, for which I could claim back a part, again with calculations and form-filling. Weekly records consisted of working out from the day sheets for the restaurant and the bakery how many hours each person had worked, and then calculating with the Inland Revenue tables their tax and insurance. Many people's hours and days varied from week to week, so there was no quick way of doing this.

I could not afford help for this operation, which was made more time-consuming when the Revenue asked employers to work out family tax credits instead of doing it themselves. I was only paying myself a management fee, which started at sixty pounds a week, and rose towards the end of the twenty-five years to a hundred a week, definitely not a fortune, and leaving no leeway for extra administration costs.

The system I devised for recording wages, takings, and day-to-day cash expenses was to enter them on duplicated day sheets. At the end of each week the figures were transferred on to our computerized accounting system, Quicken. This was operated by Brenda, the book-keeper, who spent about three hours a week on this work. She also fed into the system the VATable items, making it easier to extract what we had to pay to Customs and Excise every three months. She entered the purchases we made for which we could claim back VAT, which were then balanced. We paid VAT on the sales in the Duckery restaurant, the small items sold in the craft shop, and drinks sold from the bakery. Towards the end we were paying about £12, 000 a year to the VAT man.

Our relations with the health and safety, environmental health, and weights and measures agencies were all good. This depended heavily on carrying out anything they asked us to do promptly. I knew it would make more work in the long run if we were given bad marks for not doing what we were asked. We put in barriers between the public and the moving parts of the machinery at the beginning, of course, made safe the trapdoors which were used to haul up grain, and had contracts for pest inspections, testing the scales and fire extinguishers. There were limits to where we were allowed to hold live performances and sell alcohol. All of these considerations, as well as keeping up with new legislation, took time and energy, and became more exacting as the years went by. I came to hate the hours I spent shut away in the office, when I would have liked to be milling, talking to people, putting up an exhibition, gardening, or keeping the place running smoothly without hassle, as far as possible.

Day to day repairs and maintenance of the site was another part of my job which needed constant attention and money. Every spring we had a painting programme for the interior of the mill and the Duckery. The walls inevitably picked up damp in the winter. We also replaced broken posts or rails round the car park. Floods brought down silt, and piled up debris against the fences between the two mill meadows, and we had to keep these cleared. Potholes in the car park were filled each spring, and notices renewed or repainted. The normal garden maintenance was carried out as the seasons demanded. Sheep did a good job in keeping down the grass in the meadows, but their grazing was divided between the orchard and the mill property, so there were times when we had to cut the grass, and to keep the top meadow rolled and clear of droppings before the summer outdoor performances. Winter pruning, leaf-fall clearing, planting and weeding became my enjoyable recreations with Martha until her death, and afterwards on my own. John Early was a great support, willing to take on almost anything with a cheerful face (He doesn't like ladder work, or finding mice unexpectedly!).

Maintenance on the mill itself took time and money, too. The mill stream was cleared in the summer by Phil with first Harry, and then later with teams of the young men and women who worked at the mill. Several sluice gates had to be renewed over the years, which was expensive, and gratings needed clearing regularly. Repairs and improvements were only done if they were completely necessary, because of our precarious finances. Fumigating the system for meal moth, and greasing and oiling, had to be carried out on an annual programme, and the stones had to be dressed as and when they lost their sharpness.

Amongst other activities I spent a considerable amount of time in milling, (another of the jobs I really enjoyed), and it is easy to see how a two- or three-day cycle of flour production, combined with the time involved in taking round groups of children and adults, plus what I have mentioned above, ate up my days. Phil and I sometimes went on holiday in spring or autumn. For the rest of the year I took time off for something I did not want to miss, or when the need to get away became overwhelming. On a normal working day I crossed the road at about nine in the morning, and went home for lunch at one. Then I worked in the afternoon and went home again at about five or five-thirty. I enjoyed cooking the evening meal, one of my great pleasures. The day was usually punctuated by my crossing the road for one reason or another quite a few times, as it took about a minute to get from one building to another. This routine was broken of course when people were staying or came for a meal. There was always a stream of unexpected visitors, too, and one of the pleasantest features of this life was never knowing who was going to turn up. The courtyard at the back of the Mill House was well away from the noise of the road, and of cars going in and out of the mill property. Sometimes I would stagger in on a Bank Holiday, and people would be sitting calmly in the courtyard having tea, and asking 'Are there a few people over at the mill today?' Once an American came to the door with a copy of the *New York Times*, which was carrying an article on Devon cream teas. They recommended three tea rooms in the whole of the county, including ours, and he kindly gave me his copy. Phil and Denys were reading the Sunday papers when I excitedly showed them the article. 'Oh, you must be producing something worth eating', they said. 'Perhaps we ought to try some. ' They had left it for at least ten years before they made the decision, while people on the other side of the road queued up daily with cries of delight for our cream teas!

I worked on the ordering for the Duckery with Susie. Cash payments came out of the day's takings, and were recorded on the day sheets. Cheque payments were all made by me, which with a turnover of £180,000 meant quite a few signatures. The restaurant made a good profit, and the bakery a continually increasing one. These two really kept the whole place afloat financially.

What ate up these profits was the maintenance of the site which, with meadows, waterway, garden, car park, and machinery, had large areas that did not bring in an income. The mill is a two star listed building, so the stairs cannot be altered to make access to the first and second floors any easier for elderly people to negotiate. This is a limiting factor on the numbers who can get round the mill and see it and the exhibitions. We took an income of up to £20,000 on ticket sales, which was important for our survival. We usually broke about even, with a profit or loss of about £6,000. I used to think how miraculous it was that when the annual income and expenditure gradually went up, we still maintained this same amount of profit or loss.

We did not charge a car park fee. Many locals came to buy their bread and cakes regularly, or to have a light meal or a coffee, and they certainly would not have done so if they had had to pay to park their cars every time.

Another factor in limiting the profitability of the place was that, do what you would, the numbers of people who visited went up and down according to the seasons and the weather. In January, February and March, when our little village seems muddy and remote, not many people came to see us on weekdays, though the weekends were still busy, and the spring half term brought families down from the north and east to visit their relations or stay in their holiday cottages. The locals still came regularly to buy bakery goods, and I always had a programme of evening events to carry us through. The mill is damp at that time of year, and it was important not to show crafts and paintings which could be damaged. Milling was sometimes impossible, too, because of freeze-ups or high water levels.

All in all, we lost money in the winter, and gradually built up through the rest of the year so that we could survive. There was no way that this was a commercial proposition, but I did keep it going for the full twenty-five years, with the help of an understanding bank manager and a winter overdraft. I remained determined to keep to the ethos I had started with.

As far as the allocation of the rest of my time was concerned, a job I really loved was organizing the exhibitions. I did this in the autumn and winter for the following season, and usually started by feeling in a blind panic in about September, when I might not have more than one or two exhibitions in place for the following year. As time went on, and I had more and more contacts, it did become easier, but fourteen or so slots to fill every season was quite a challenge. Autumn was also the time for doing some research for the following summer exhibition. This normally drew on some aspect of local history or the environment. I liked these exhibitions to run for the whole of the summer holidays, because then I had so much to do that I always felt I was on a roller coaster, or shooting rapids, for six weeks. The idea of changing over an exhibition with all that was entailed, such as sending out press releases, private view invitations and posters, setting up and taking down a previous show, and liaising with artists – this would have been too time-consuming at that time of year. I tried to keep my diary clear for day-to-day events and crises, and I kept myself available to slot into any job which might need doing. On Sundays it was often washing up in the Duckery, as it was extremely difficult to gauge how many staff were needed for the busy parts of the day. During the rest of the week I might get involved in sorting out a drainage problem, or milling extra flour (at a time when the water table was at its lowest). A group would suddenly arrive unexpectedly, and want to be taken on a tour. One Bank Holiday Monday the clotted cream delivery did not arrive, and Denys and I bought up all the clotted cream in Exmouth's Tesco, pots and pots of it! We normally went through forty pounds or so of the stuff in a Bank Holiday weekend. I used to think about the harm that was doing to all those different people's arteries, and after quite a short time could hardly look at a tub of clotted cream!

Another time, the key to the shop safe got dropped into the stream by someone hurrying across the wooden bridge on a Bank Holiday Monday. No transactions could take place! My cousin Jeremy was staying with us for Easter, and he spent an hour or so in the stream bed below the wheel and actually, most miraculously, found it. It had been washed twenty yards or so downstream.

In the last year of my time at the mill, we broke the pattern of expenditure and income which had been built up over such a long time while we searched for a future. Now, I am glad to say, the mill's future looks good.